Beyond the Four Walls

Beyond the Four Walls

The Rising Ministry and Spirituality of Hip-hop

By Walter Lizando Hidalgo-Olivares

Edited by Dorsett Clark Davis, M.A. and Evans Erilus, M.S.
Graphic Design by Rammer Martínez Sánchez at SmokyMirrors.com
Photography by Anibal Farran at newyorkedition.net

authorHOUSE®

AuthorHouse™
1663 Liberty Drive
Bloomington, IN 47403
www.authorhouse.com
Phone: 1-800-839-8640

First published by AuthorHouse   06/29/2011

ISBN: 978-1-4634-1259-3 (sc)
ISBN: 978-1-4634-1258-6 (dj)
ISBN: 978-1-4634-1964-6 (ebk)

Library of Congress Control Number: 2011910312

Printed in the United States of America

Any people depicted in stock imagery provided by Thinkstock are models, and such images are being used for illustrative purposes only.
Certain stock imagery © Thinkstock.

This book is printed on acid-free paper.

This book is dedicated to the Creator of all things. Through Him, I have had the joy of walking, breathing and seeing all of the remarkable things that this earth has to offer, including a loving family, amazing friends, and the unforgettable experiences of traveling to many different places in the world.

Special Thanks to:

First and foremost I would like to thank the Almighty God who makes ALL things possible! With every breath that I take and every step that I make, I do it all for His glory! To ALL of my family (nuclear and extended) and my friends (close and far). I also would like to thank what we in the Hip-hop world and the streets refer to as the haters. Shout out to you guys as well!

I also would like to thank Union Theological Seminary, Columbia University, Northeastern University, Touro College, Marymount Manhattan College, Mount Pleasant High School in Rhode Island, Bishop McVinney Middle School in Rhode Island, The Columbia University Spectator, The Ecumenical Water Network in Geneva, Switzerland, The School of Peace in Bogota, Colombia, The Cultural House organization in Medellin, Colombia, The Bedford Hills College Program, The Hispanic Summer Program, The Community Ministers Program at Judson Memorial Church, Critical Resistance organization in the Bronx, Rev. Dr. Martin Luther King Jr.'s Poor People's Campaign, The Industrial Areas Foundation, Urban Word, Picture the Homeless organization in New York City, Bread for the World, The Poverty Initiative at Union Theological Seminary, The New Sanctuary Movement of New York City, Youth Ministries for Peace and Justice in the South Bronx, Brick Presbyterian Church in Manhattan, Judson Memorial Church of Manhattan, The Hip-hop Church of Harlem, The Riverside Church in Harlem, The Oratory Church of St. Boniface in Brooklyn, Our Lady of Mount Carmel Church in Rhode Island, Praise Tabernacle Church in Cranston, Rhode Island, The First Presbyterian Church of Miami, Tha House in Chicago, The Latino Pastoral Action Center in the Bronx, Rev. Raymond Rivera, Rev. Dr. Donna Schaper, Rev. Howard Moody, Rev. Dr. Samuel Cruz, Rev. Dr. Josef Sorett, Rev. Dr. Daisy Machado, Dr. Gary Dorrien, Rev. Dr. Hal Taussig, Rev. Dr. Christopher Morse, Father Roger Haight, Father Hugo, Father Loft, Rev. J. Lee Hill, Jr., Rev. Bob Coleman, Alain Silverio, Nina Saxon, Rev. Osagyefo Sekou, Professor Janet Walton, Professor Willie Baptist, Dr. James Cone, Dr. Neil Altman, etc . . . .

I would also like to thank the following Hip-hop folks and resources that have inspired me personally (in no particular order): Danny AKA Mystery, Majesty, Omar Fisher, Joseph AKA Joker, Spirit Child, my cousin Robby, Din Tolbert, Honorable George Martinez, Rasheed Goodlowe, Solomon Starr, Da T.R.U.T.H, DJ Nocturnal, DJ Raw, DJ Lefty, DJ Pooh, DJ Grandmaster Flash, DJ Premier, DJ Ed Nice, DJ Fred the Great, Gang Starr, The Wu-Tang Clan, Boot Camp Clik, B.U.M.S., Mobb Deep, Mase, Canibus, The Notorious BIG, Nas, The Fugees, The Lost Boys, Jay-Z, Salt N Pepa, The LOX, Lauryn Hill, MC Lyte, Big Punisher, DMX, Beanie Sigel, Joell Ortiz, Rock Steady, Redman, Snoop Dogg, Lupe Fiasco, Dead Prez, Big L, KRS-One, Tupac Shakur, Rakim, Matisyahu, De La Soul, Black Sheep, Five Percenters, Universal Zulu Nation, Queen Latifah, Afrika Bambaataa, Black Moon, The Sugar Hill Gang, LL Cool J, Melle Mel, Free, The Roots, Rah Digga, Eve, Naughty by Nature, Channel Live, AZ, Nature, Busta Rhymes, EPMD, NWA, Dr. Dre, Eminem, Foxy Brown, Heltah Skeltah, Public Enemy, Black Starr, De La Soul, Pete Rock and CL Smooth, 'Lil Kim, Jeru the Damaja, Outkast, Goodie Mob, Run DMC, Beatnuts, A Tribe Called Quest, Bone Thugs-n-Harmony, Royce Da 5'9, Scarface, Big Daddy Kane, Immortal Technique, Mos Def, Common, Talib Kweli, Hot 106.3 FM (Providence, RI), Hot 97.1 FM (New York, NY), and 94.5 FM (Boston, MA), etc . . . .

Thank you to the following music genres that have inspired me throughout my life: The Spoken Word Movement, Jazz, Alternative Rock, Salsa, Merengue, Techno, Free style, Classical, Marimba, Reggae, Rhumba, Dance Hall Reggae, Soca, Cumbia, Rhythm and Blues, Gospel, The Underground Hip-hop Movement, and of course, Hip-Hop!

Thank you to my editors, Evans Erilus and Dorsett Clark Davis, my graphic designer, Rammer Martínez Sánchez, and my photographer Anibal Farran.

Very Special thanks to ALL the people that I met throughout this process who I forgot to mention: youth, young adults, MC's, DJ's, B-boy's and B-girl's alike, poets, graffiti artist, spoken word artist, students, not-for-profit organizations, ministers, professors, community organizers, spiritual leaders and activists. All of you have inspired me to continue to fight for social justice, both locally and globally.

Contents

"Now there are varieties of gifts, but the same Spirit; and there are varieties of services, but the same Lord; and there are varieties of activities, but it is the same God who activates all of them in everyone. To each is given the manifestation of the Spirit for the common good."

—1 Corinthians 12:4-7

PREFACE

When a lively mind encounters a lively subject, music breaks out of its neighborhood, goes on safari, or develops a new multi-generational, multi-income housing project where the elevators work and the syncopation sizzles. Hip-hop hops fences – it mixes musical metaphors; to it, old musical forms feel like last year's blue jeans. This book is as happy as a new pair of well-fitting jeans.

Hip-hop is non-denominational, while being deeply affiliated. Its forms make believe they are formless. A traditional history of its form has now developed, allowing us to see its version of a sacrament, a ritual, even a tradition.

Body is the boldness of Hip-hop. A lot of people talk about embodiment, theologically. Hip-hop does it. A lot of people talk about the incarnation – encarnación – as the bodied bread of Jesus, whose blood poured out into a hip, a hop, a historical happening. When you see someone on the subway with Hip-hop playing in their ears, you see shoulders spiritually shaking their souls. Some will confuse that with Eucharist; all will know it as embodiment.

When you leave this book, both your body and your soul will be refreshed – and in motion.

Reverend Doctor Donna Schaper
Senior Minister of Judson Memorial Church in New York City
Author of numerous books, most recently, "A Study Guide to Howard Thurman"

PRELUDE

The summer of 2007 was coming to an end and I was about to embark on one of life's most challenging roads: graduate school. Not knowing exactly what I was getting into, I decided to attend a two-year graduate program to study theology (more specifically, Church History and Society) at Union Theological Seminary (UTS) at Columbia University in New York City. What I, a Roman Catholic, heterosexual, first-generation Latino man from the South Side of Providence, Rhode Island experienced in and out of these academic walls would eventually change my life forever.

While studying at UTS, I began to see how God was bringing me together with other people of diverse backgrounds to discuss the common realities of our times—poverty, homelessness, racism, etc. Over time, it became clear to me the importance of having a dialogue with the very thing that defines us as humans—our society. Consequently, I made the decision to break through the "bubble" or "box" that I was living in order to reach out and help (more broadly) my brothers and sisters. This epiphany was the reason I came to admire the efforts that are being made by the Ecumenical Movement.

Ecumenical by definition suggest a unity between the various denominations that exist within Christianity. One can go as far as to say this unifying ideology includes other world religions as well, such as Buddhism, Islam, Judaism, Hinduism, etc. Regardless of the definition of Ecumenical, love of God, love of self and love of neighbor are considered to be fundamental characteristics of every faith because they serve as emblems for justice, peace, truth and unity!

For me, togetherness is God. But to come together, we first need to understand that God has presented Himself to people based on their own sociopolitical, economical, historical and cultural realities. In other words, God speaks to us in different ways but He expects all of us to do the same thing—to bring God's Kingdom a little closer to earth.

Throughout my time at UTS, I've learned that God can be encountered in many places outside of the church. For example, I was able to experience God's presence in many "unusual" places like supervised therapy sessions, travel seminar classes to places like Colombia in South America, and weekly meetings to discuss community-related issues by a group of women who were formerly incarcerated—just to name a few. Yes, Church is a place where we can talk to and encounter God. However, I would be lying to myself if I were to say that God's spirit is limited to the four walls of the Church and therefore is unable to reach out to the broader secular places of our world.

For me, there is no separation between God and human beings no matter where they are, who they are and how they do worship. It is what I perceive to be God's spirit that brings people together to talk about life, happiness, sadness, anger, hope and love. In my view, one of the best platforms for intersecting God with our society is Hip-hop music and culture.

Hip-hop has always served as a platform for people of diverse backgrounds, especially those that are living in the margins of our societies. Its dialogical style of rhyming, free-styling, graffiti art work, dance and DJ-ing are like magnets to the millions of people who embrace it. When openly received, it creates a spiritual, sociopolitical and grassroots-centered consciousness that unifies all of God's people.

Hip-hop has had such an impact in our world because it has given countless silent voices the ability to be heard and to be part of this historical meta-narrative. Throughout my existence here on earth, I have seen the positive influences of Hip-hop music and culture in the following ways: graffiti art work to demonstrate the oppressive/negative side of politics in Geneva, Switzerland; alternative programs for Colombian inner-city youth who are struggling with guerilla army recruitment; and continuous contributions to academia using performances and workshops to convey lessons to students in schools like Columbia University.

In reality, this book can be interpreted in many ways—all depending on the reader of course. For some, it may be viewed as an interesting read while for others it may be viewed as wishful thinking. But for many, including myself, this is a book about how Hip-hop helps to bring the spirit of God to youth ministers, professors, clergy, politicians, activists, not-for-profit organizations, academic institutions, prisons, the projects, the Gaza strip, Africa, Asia, Europe, the Americas, to the elders, to the youth, etc.

To a larger extent, this book serves as a testimony to my experiences growing up listening to Hip-hop and living in an environment similar to that which is portrayed in many songs in the Hip-Hop culture. When I think about my experiences growing up and my experiences at UTS (especially the research that I did for my masters thesis on Hip-hop), I would say that I bring to the table the best of both worlds—the scholarly knowledge that is learned in the academic world and the wisdom that is acquired in the streets.

Because of Hip-hop, I have been given the opportunity to visit many places throughout the world and to meet so many incredible human beings. For all these opportunities and more, I thank God for bringing Hip-hop into my life!

THE MIC

All I need is one Mic . . . . that's what Nas said/

But this one Mic is what moves large crowds like World Cup matches/

That ignites a fire . . . whenever these words touch the torch of the Apollo/

These so-called "rappers" rhyme a tough talk . . . but never walk inside
my ghetto/

Cause my rhymes don't hold grudges . . . so these words I release and just
let 'em go/

And move freely . . . like the wind that blows my hair whenever I'm in
Chicago/

As I spit the truth . . . . the kind that shines light into the darkest of
places/

I turn the hood . . . . into gatherings where youth seek a safe haven/

Cause when Hip-hop married purpose . . . it only conceived a
revolution/

That's why I'm like an asexual animal . . . producing my own next
generation/

I'm from places where . . . . . the elders pray for souls beyond moderation/

Where these gangs are left with no right . . . sense of direction/

But never in a state of depression . . . that could only cause a
commotion/

But this *is* Hip-hop . . . our words hold sound hostage and stir-up a motion/

So take a deep ride in my sea of thoughts . . . . where you might just catch me drifting/

Where I roam (Rome) the earth and speak publicly like Paul the Apostle . . . . just to see if Italy was listening/

Cause I'm more than what you are witnessing . . . cause aint nothing defining my soul/

I just plant Jesus' mustard seed by tomatoes . . . so it can ketchup (catch up) . . . and grow on fertile soil/

I speak for the whole . . . not the divided . . . my life yields infinite factors/

With so many chapters . . . . my book mark reads "see you right afterwards"/

So I just prefer living it . . . only to hope that tomorrow I get to do it again/

Cause only God is the author of my life . . . I'm just reading it!/

By Walter Hidalgo
Performed at Union Theological Seminary at Columbia University in New York City on April 20, 2010

INTRODUCTION

Most people cannot deal with the possible fact that what they are is not all of what they are getting. That there is a deeper, faster, stronger reality that can actually override the mechanics of their known physical universe and its laws. That thing might not actually be the way we think they are. For most people such a revelation is indeed scary and not even to be discussed. But for a select few, such a revelation is inspiring and encourages such people to learn more, seek more and live more.

—**KRS-One**
The Gospel of Hip-hop

The year was 1990, and I remember sitting outside of my front porch watching my next door neighbor's break dancing to Afrika Bambaataa and the Soul Sonic Force's hit song, *Planet Rock.* For me, this form of dancing, which was unlike any other style that I'd ever seen before, was not only difficult to mimic but fun to watch. At the same time, I recall seeing this flamboyant car with 18 inch rims riding down our street playing Rakim and Eric B's song, *Let the Rhythm Hit 'Em.* It occurred to me that everyone was "feeling" this particular song because it was not the first time I heard it that day, let alone that week.

I was only eight years old and still new to this music called Hip-hop. But I nevertheless fell in love with it—and still love it today. As, a first generation Latino, born and raised in a predominately Black and Latino/a city (the South Side of Providence, Rhode Island), I can say that an overwhelming majority of my Black and Latino/a brothers and sisters also fell in love with this music because it was, well, everywhere!

For me, it was the 1990's when Hip-hop began to shine. I refer to this era as the "Golden Years" of Hip-hop because it was the time when some of the best rappers, or MC's ("Mic Check," "Master of Ceremony", or "Move the Crowd"), of all time came out. Some of those artists included the following: Notorious BIG, Tupac Shakur, Big Daddy Kane, Big Punisher, Nas, Brand Nubian, Rakim, The Lox, Immortal Technique, Free, Canibus, Pharoahe Monch, The Wu-Tang Clan, Kool G Rap, The Roots, Gang Starr, AZ, Jay-Z, Outcast, Black Sheep, Black Moon, Mos Def, Lauryn Hill, Common, Goodie Mob, Capone N Noreaga, etc. It was these MC's who defined what it meant to be a minority living in one of the many urbanized communities in the United States. And so, places like the South Side of Providence, where there is a high minority population, became just one of many other cities that gravitated to this music.

But what was once a representation of various communities throughout the United States exemplifying cohesiveness soon became replaced by monetary endeavors. The rebuilding of decaying neighborhoods was replaced with platinum chains, and songs like "Unity" by Queen Latifah were replaced with songs like "Five Star Chick" by Yo Gotti.

Yet despite the capitalistic, misogynistic and materialistic infusion that Hip-hop music sometimes produces by way of four-minute music videos and multi-million dollar radio stations; Hip-hop continues to inspire millions. Unlike some critics who interpret Hip-hop as being altogether evil, I, on the other hand, view Hip-hop as a genre of music *and* a culture that creates a platform for anyone (no matter the age, sex, race, class or creed of the individual) to express themselves in light of their own social reality. It is an art form that can be used as a medium to create a public discourse that spreads sociopolitical awareness, community activism, and in many instances, helps to generate a more meaningful relationship with God based on this "call" towards social action.

Now, you might be asking yourself, "which God is he referring to?" Well, realistically speaking, Hip-hop has no particular religious affiliation, or devotion to a particular kind of God for that matter. However, during its early-to-middle stages, it appeared to have some influence from the Five Percenters. The Five Percenters are an offshoot of the Nation of Islam.[1] This group (which holds its genesis in Harlem) taught their youth, particularly African-Americans, that since they were made in the image of God, they are in fact Gods themselves. In other words, by believing that they themselves hold the same (exact) characteristics as God, or

---

[1]   For further discussion of this topic, please see Michael Muhammad Knight, *The Five Percenters: Islam, Hip-hop and the Gods of New York* (Oxford, England: Oneworld Publications, 2007).

Allah, anything that they put their minds to here on earth can and will be accomplished.

In addition to their theological contributions, it was the knowledge of the Five Percenters, among other things, that laid the foundation of Hip-hip's lyrical metaphors, punch lines and street slang. For example, the words "Peace," "Cipher" and "Word is born," are but a few of the same words that make up the science, or doctrines, of the Five Percenters. For those who are not experts or familiar with Hip-hop, these words (with the exception of the word "peace") are nothing more than street slang with no substance behind them.

But the truth is, although Hip-hop has no official affiliation with any particular religion or doctrine, reference of God, or Allah, in Hip-hop lyrics is as common as these MC's who produce them. Looking ahead and beyond I will show how Hip-hop is used as an instrument for the glory of God, but more specifically, the teachings of Jesus Christ. As a believer in the teachings of Jesus and the transformative power of the spirit of God, it is only right that I approach Hip-hop from this particular vantage point.

From left to right: Richard "KOM3" Scott of the Breaks Kru, Olivia Martinez, violinist for BR & Timebomb, Steve, Me, Rammer Martínez Sánchez, my graphic designer, Luis "Vanquish" Cruz of Evolution/No Control, Bryan "Prophet" Pacheco of Evolution/No Control, Ivan "Iceman" Espinal of Breaks Kru and Evolution/No Control, and Anibal Farran, my photographer.

Now, this is not to conclude that Hip-hop, from a global perspective, is imperialistic with an agenda for power. On the contrary, unlike those individuals or groups that have used the Gospels to spread Christianity in an unjustifiable way to the non-believers (like the Spanish did to the Indigenous populations of Latin America, or the Manifest Destiny ideology that was used by Anglo-Saxons in order to justify their expansion westward in North America): Hip-hop did not globalize in order to colonize! Instead, Hip-hop came to the streets as a way of organizing diverse peoples from the community through an alternative form of communication—without brute force.

This convergence of diverse groups is what has led me to write about Hip-hop. Seeing Hip-hop's efforts in trying to create a dialogue between localized communities has demonstrated to me a collective consciousness that is not only based on their love of the culture, but also those same social injustices that were destroying their respective communities.

For example, at the turn of the 21st Century my alma mater, Northeastern University, conducted a case study where they found high incidents of racial profiling in and around the city of Providence. The Institute on Race and Justice and the College of Criminal Justice found that in Providence, "56.3% of all traffic stops were of non-White motorists compared to a non-White driving population estimate of 32.2% for the city, yielding a disparity of 24.1%." [2] This report, which at the time I had the privilege of being part of, did not, however, talk about the various other injustices that were occurring in Providence, such as poverty and poor school systems.

The racial profiling typical of my neighborhood was also being felt in other urban communities, such as the South Bronx borough of New York City. I will discuss this in more depth in the following chapter. But for right now, it's important to see how racial profiling was affecting minority urban youth because I too have been the victim of unlawful stops and misconducts by the Providence Police. Unfortunately, racial profiling was just one of many prejudices that affected minority youth in urban cities. Some of those other injustices included the following: gentrification, drugs, corporate greed, government corruption, broken families, youth rebellion, racism and environmental injustices, to just name a few.

---

[2]   Amy Farrell and Jack McDevitt, "Rhode Island Traffic Stop Statistics Act Final Report," *Northeastern University Institute on Race and Justice,* 31 December 2002, *Data Collection Resource Center* [database on-line]; accessed on March 3, 2009.

These trends that were occurring almost daily soon became the impetus for a common consciousness manifesting itself among marginalized youth of distinct racial, sexual and class identifications. In other words, diversity, along with all the other "-isms" that it suggests, started to become irrelevant once individual youths in urban cities began to realize that their problems were also everyone else's problems (e.g. poverty, police mistrust, etc.).

Eventually, the realization of these common destructive forces resulted in the transformation of a silenced minority in the South Bronx into an unsurpassable communal testimony that would soon be heard in other cities in the United States—and the world.

As I mentioned previously, the Hip-hop that I grew up listening to had become more than just entertainment; it was a public demonstration that could be seen all over the city. You can see it in the walls of buildings as a result of graffiti artist, in the break dancing moves on the streets corners, and in the gatherings of MC's and DJ's at block parties.[3]

As a practicing Roman Catholic Christian and youth minister, these public venues made me rethink and re-imagine what our churches not only look like, but what their functions are in the broader society. I made this connection based on my lifelong observation and participation in the Hip-hop movement and culture, which ultimately touched my heart and moved my spirit to do something not just for myself, but for my community. Over time, I found myself gathering around MC's of all walks of life who were using this genre to convey words of self-expression, hope and a deep criticism of those same systems—government, law enforcement, institutionalized religion, etc.—that were oppressing them.

I saw churches that were being developed in the streets as they gathered people in the name of God through the use of the streets' native tongue—Hip-hop. This gathering of "Hip-hoppers" in the community reminded me of the early churches of antiquity that Paul the Apostle tried to establish in and around the Mediterranean Sea. These early churches consisted of groups of diverse communities who would gather for fellowship and dialogue about their daily lives and God while enjoying a meal. I

---

[3] A Block Party is a large public party in which many members of a single neighborhood congregate, either to observe an event of some importance or simply for mutual enjoyment. The name comes from the form of the party, which often involves closing an entire city block to vehicle traffic. Block parties gained popularity in the United States during the 1970s.

take this viewpoint of the church primarily from Shawn Madigan's book, *Spirituality Rooted in Liturgy;* at the same time, I take my understanding of these Hip-hop gatherings as early church replicas in respect to Professor Roger Haight's book, *Christian Community in History: Volume I.* The latter version of the church is the reason I am approaching both Hip-hop's history and church history from a more sociological perspective.

Another way of viewing the church comes from a well known theologian, Reverend Dr. Hal Taussig. Dr. Taussig, a visiting Professor of New Testament at Union Theological Seminary in New York City, has a written a book entitled, *In the Beginning was the Meal: Social Experimentation and Early Christian Identity.* This book describes the early churches of the followers of The Way (the first name given to the early Christians) as being nothing more than gatherings of people of diverse backgrounds who would sit around eating a meal while publicly discussing their socio-political, economical, theological and gender-relational context in accordance with the teachings of Jesus Christ. Without a doubt, this socio-historical interpretation of the church by Dr. Taussig stands in juxtaposition with my view of Hip-hop and the church. I will explain what I mean by this in subsequent chapters.

This brings me to our second component of Hip-hop culture, its spirituality. When MC's or graffiti artists express their contextual realities using the Hip-hop culture, they in turn create a space that freely invites people into an emotional and invigorating place. This space becomes more intensified in the public places of the world as opposed to the domesticated and exclusiveness of a spirit that is trapped indoors. Being out in the public's eye; however, suggests that the spirit is more inclusive. It also demonstrates to those around it that a collective emotion is powerful because it allows *all* types of people from the community to come together and experience it as well.

Danny AKA Mystery spitting rhymes to the youth at the Chad Brown
Projects in Providence, Rhode Island.

So when we talk about the role of spirituality *within* history, specifically
Hip-hop's timeline, we are referring to the *same* spirit that has helped
countless people to seek a deeper relationship with God.

Before His journey back home, Jesus told his disciples that they
themselves would be guided by the spirit—the very same spirit that
enabled Jesus to create miracles. Unfortunately, in the midst of exegetical
research in academia and the overall inability to believe in spirituality due
to its lack of rational understanding, our interpretation of spirituality has
become misconstrued. As a result, the little miracles spirituality can create
on a daily basis are overlooked.

So when I talk about spirituality, I am not referring to the ability to
walk on water nor am I talking about a divine encounter so-to-speak. I
define spirituality as something that is manifested in places where open
dialogue and reflection are respected. In this way, the spiritual element that
is associated with Hip-hop music and culture is not merely a peripheral,
incidental or personal quality of Hip-hop, but rather the foundation upon
which youth and young adults [particularly those that are left in the margins
of society] are motivated to seek a deeper relationship with God. This

in turn helps to alter the individuals' self-identity while simultaneously creating a collective consciousness that promotes social transformation.

The spirit of Hip-hop, therefore, is something that comes to life whenever people come together to discuss, or rhyme, their own interpretation of their existential surroundings. The example I mentioned earlier regarding racial profiling in Providence helps to reinforce this association between peoples' sociological hardships and spirituality. This also helps us to make sense of how the subjective perspective of an individual's experiences living in the "ghetto" transitions itself to a more dialectic testimony.

The bringing together of people living under oppressive conditions *is* what is collectively helping youth and young adults establish a more theological framework of God by interpreting God's participation in their society through the lens of Hip-hop culture and its various public ministries to the non-believers.

Me performing at Columbia University.

Throughout my graduate school research, as well as my own personal experiences growing up with the Hip-hop culture, I have come to the conclusion that it's those churches, which are overwhelmingly Pentecostal and non-denominational, that are at the forefront of utilizing Hip-hop culture as a way to draw youth and young adults living in the margins into a relationship with God. In turn, these gatherings reflect the true meaning of the church that I alluded to earlier by catering to the spiritual and ministerial needs of "even the least of these."

Whatever your conclusions on Hip-hop may be, Hip-hop culture is in fact helping us to create a "space" that binds marginalized youth and young adults together into fellowship, dialogue, worship, social critique and of course, spirituality—rendering it one of the real churches of our time. But more importantly, Hip-hop culture is turning us back to the core principles of Christianity—or any other religion for that matter—by promoting love, comm*unity*, hope, peace, joy and justice. These principles have a tendency to come to life whenever there is open dialogue amongst people of different walks of life. Paulo Freire, who wrote the famous book, *The Pedagogy of the Oppressed,* defines dialogue eloquently when he says that "dialogue is a hermeneutic of *humility*, where neither side projects ignorance onto the other in order to assert its own absoluteness, ignorant of limitations. Rather, both sides practice humility by acknowledging their limitations, leaving space for the choice of the other while also being open to be transformed by it."

Spaces that allow an open dialogue for social critique have always served as places where we experience this sense of humanity and fragileness that is naturally embedded in us and therefore reminds us of our absence of something much bigger than our own selves—God. The church *is supposed* to—and to an extent it does—provide this kind of environment for their communities.

Yet, in my experiences, I have found the secular gathering places of the world to do the same thing, if not more so. Places like an Alcoholics Anonymous group, youth break dancing in protest of unfair employment wages, group therapy sessions, MC battles to raise money for schools, or higher education courses with titles such as Post-Racial Thought and Social Ethics as Social Criticism. All of these spaces have provided human beings the ability to encounter spirituality as a result of their souls communicating with each other in an open safe space of dialectic critique and love for justice.

Yet, despite all this, there continues to be many churches, clergy men and women, institutions of higher learning and youth ministry programs that disapprove of Hip-hop's culture because it's too loud and outspoken, and they accuse it of having an inherently evil spirit. Well, it's important to understand what Paul the Apostle said: we should be conscious of both good spirits and bad spirits. And quite frankly, there are bad spirits in Hip-hop culture, such as the overuse of foul language, the degradation of women and the promotion of material wealth. However, that *is not* the Hip-hop that I am referring to; the Hip-hop that I know has always been positive and best summarized by one of my favorite MC's of all time, KRS-One. He says Hip-hop is about "Peace, Love, Unity and having fun!"

So before we even begin to demonize Hip-hop, we must not forget the great things and great spirits that have come from it. Because realistically speaking, the same evil spirits that are found in Hip-hop can also be found in Christian or other religious circles, or for that matter, our government, schools and criminal justice systems. Therefore, when we think about Hip-hop culture it is important that we *go beyond Hip-hop* and consider the bigger picture that is being painted before our very own eyes.

My passion for Hip-hop combined with my faith in God is what pushes me to encourage our leaders—specifically our pastors, youth ministers, congregants, lay workers and seminarians—to consider utilizing Hip-hop as a way to draw these marginalized youth together in solidarity, so that in time, they too can develop a more intimate, and spiritual, relationship with God. I am confident that this can happen because I have seen it happen time after time. And now, I believe, the time has come: We must let the world know that this music genre known as Hip-hop is not going away but is staying put. Because where there is struggle, hope and comm*unity*, there is the spirit of God . . . . there is . . . . Hip-hop!

Let us begin.

CHAPTER 1:

In the Beginning, there was Hip-hop:

Looking at Hip-hop from a Sociohistorical Lens

Hip means to know
It's a form of intelligence/
To be hip is to be up'date and relevant/
Hop is a form of movement/
You can't just observe a hop
You got to hop up and do it/
Hip and Hop is more than music/
Hip is the knowledge
Hop is the movement/
Hip and Hop is intelligent movement/
All relevant movement
We selling the music/
So write this down on your black books and journals/
Hip-hop culture is eternal/
Run and tell all your friends
An ancient civilization has been born again/
It's a fact!

I come back!
Cause I'm not in the physical/
I create myself man I live in the spiritual/
I come back through the cycles of life/
If you been here once you gone be here twice/
So I tell you!
I come back!
Cause you must learn too/
Hip-hop culture is eternal/

Hip-hop!
Her **I**nfinite **P**ower
Helping **O**ppressed **P**eople/
We are unique and unequaled/ . . . .
Hip-Hop!
Holy **I**ntegrated **P**eople
Having **O**mnipresent **P**ower/
The watchman's in the tower/ of . . .

Hip-hop!
The response of cosmic consciousness . . . .
To our condition as . . . .
Hip-hop!
We gotta think about the children we bringing up/
When Hip and Hop means intelligence springing up/
We singing what?
Sickness, Hatred, Ignorance, and Poverty or Health/
Love, Awareness, and Wealth/
Follow me!

—KRS-One
From the song entitled *Hip-hop Lives (I Come Back)*

*During the 1980's the rich got richer and the poor got poorer,
unemployment was high, and racial tensions were even higher. People
of color were angry and the spirit of protest hung thick in the air.
Armed with lessons learned from their parents' and grandparents' era
when southern African-Americans inspired millions of red, brown
and yellow people all over the world to rebel against oppression, Black
students and their supporters once again took the streets.*

—Tayannah Lee McQuillar and Brother J of the X-Clan
*When Rap Music Had a Conscience: The Artists, Organizations
and Historic Events that Inspired and Influenced the Golden Age
of Hip-Hop from 1987 to 1996*

"Hip-hop aint dead it just had a heart attack."

—Lil Wayne
From the song entitled *Last of a Dying
Breed*

There are so many ways we can look at, or better yet interpret, Hip-hop's history and its key players. But realistically speaking, like any other history, it is difficult to capture *everything* that was happening throughout this period of time, not to mention the countless unsung heroes that have contributed to this culture and have yet to receive their recognition—the people who provided technical, educational, and inspirational support that inspired Hip-hop voices and performers to reach a level beyond their own potential.

Recognizing the "players" of the Hip-hop culture is critical. However, that is only half the battle. But in fact, it is the arena that the players "play" in that is just as important whenever we talk about youth in the Hip-hop culture. In other words, it is in the environment of our youth, or what Pierre Burdeux calls ones' habitus, that makes the Hip-hop culture a stepping ground for both subjective and social observation and transformation.

Exploring the urbanization of any city in the United States, or the world for that matter, requires deep analysis in its growing populations, real estate development, political application and its media outlets. Why? Because it was in those elements of the urban infrastructure that helped produce Hip-hop culture over forty years ago. The people who were involved in the development of Hip-hop culture experienced many urban sociological challenges, which can be seen in the way youth express themselves (i.e. constructing a beat, fashion, rhyming delivery), and is also based on their geographical and social location.[4]

Gentrification, racism, culture shock and xenophobia are a few of those social problems present in and around the South Bronx in the 1970's, 1980's and to some extent, the 1990's and which led to the beginnings and rebuilding of Hip-hop culture and pride. Together these problems created a social space for youth to express themselves in light of their own social reality.

---

[4] For further discussion on this, please see Emmett George Price, *Hip-Hop Culture* (Santa Barbara, California: ABC-CLIO Inc., 2006).

Graffiti art work in Washington Heights, Manhattan.

Clive Campbell, known to many as DJ Kool Herc,[5] was faced with this social space when he and his family immigrated to New York City from Jamaica. While living in the Bronx, he innovated a new style by incorporating his Jamaican style of DJ-ing into the various styles and cultures present by reciting improvised rhymes over dubbed versions of Reggae records. DJ Kool Herc chanted over the instrumental or percussion sections of popular songs of the day (disco, rock n roll and rhythm and blues). Because these breaks were relatively short, it provided the best dance beats and therefore learned to extend them indefinitely by using an audio mixer and two identical records and continuously replacing and repeating

---

[5]   For further discussion on this topic, please see Steven Hagger. *Hip Hop: The Illustrated History of Break Dancing, Rap Music, and Graffiti* (New York: St. Martin's Press, 1984).

the desired segment. He did this by isolating the instrumental portion of the record which emphasized the drum beat—the "break"—and from there, he switched from one break to another to yet another, allowing dancers to keep on dancing and eventually competing with each other. This is why DJ Kool Herc called his dancers "*break* dancers."[6]

Unfortunately, New Yorkers weren't into Reggae at the time. But when DJ Kool Herc combined his style of DJ-ing with his Jamaican cultural influence, specifically his love for Reggae music; it helped to create (and diversify) Hip-hop music through the sounds and voices of countless diverse and marginalized youth in the streets of the South Bronx.[7]

KRS-One, an MC, scholar and now motivational speaker from the South Bronx, is another witness to this socio-historical revolution. Another example of a New York immigrant who had embraced his own Jamaican roots and influences, KRS-One talks about the history of Hip-hop in a similar fashion:

"A product of cross-cultural integration, rap is deeply rooted within ancient African culture and oral tradition. Hip-hop is believed to have originated in the Bronx by a Jamaican DJ named Kool Herc. Kool Herc's style of deejaying (DJ-ing) involved reciting rhymes over instrumentals. At house parties, Kool Herc would rap with the microphone, using a myriad of in-house references. Duplicates of Kool Herc's house parties soon drifted through Brooklyn and Manhattan. Kool Herc and other block party DJ's helped spread the message of hip-hop around town and spawned tons of followers."[8]

---

[6]   Break dancing, also called breaking, or b-boying is a street dance style that evolved as part of the hip hop movement among African American, Asian and Puerto Rican youths in Manhattan and the South Bronx of New York City during the early 1970s. It is normally danced to electro or hip hop music, often remixed to prolong the breaks, and is a well-known hip hop dance style.

[7]   Jeff, Chang. *Can't Stop, Won't Stop: A History of the Hip-hop Generation* (New York: St. Martin's Press, 2005), 68-72.

[8]   Henry Adaso, ed., "A Brief History of Hip-Hop and Rap," *About.Com: Rap/ Hip-hop*, [Database-on-line]; available from http://www.about.com; Internet; Accessed 8 December 2008.

Over the course of its years, Hip-hop has grown in popularity because its visible force offers young urban minority New Yorkers a chance to come together freely and express themselves. This form of expression can be seen in all of the elements of Hip-hop culture: graffiti, break dancing, DJ-ing and of course MC-ing. However, as a spoken word artist myself, I see the MC-ing element of Hip-hop—its "word"—as contributing most to the gathering of countless marginalized minority youth in the South Bronx—mainly West Indians, Latino/as and African-Americans. Hip-hop, and its various elements, represented for them (and me) a culture that was living in consort with its socio-historical realty.[9]

The culture of Hip-hop acted like of force of gravity to those who lived in and around the South Bronx because it was performed in public venues of the city, the streets. These public demonstrations and block parties had created a fellowship among diverse neighbors by employing language and sentiment of struggle, hope, liberation and God. This spiritual force soon spread out beyond the context of the Bronx and was first introduced to me in Providence, Rhode Island in the 1990's.

Consequently, what DJ Kool Herc (and myself) experienced in the 1990's in the South Bronx is, more or less, what the other fathers of Hip-hop experienced in the beginning of these Hip-hop community gatherings—or block parties. These parties brought with them diversity and different perspectives that helped to embody and grow the Hip-hop culture. It brought other Bronx residents together, people like Afrika Bambaataa, founder of the Zulu Nation[10] and the son of parents from Jamaica and Barbados; Barbados-born Joseph Saddler, known to many as DJ Grandmaster Flash—one of the pioneers in the art of DJ-ing; and finally, DJ Love Bug Starski, who is known for DJ-ing at Harlem World, a famous venue in New York City that hosted MC battles ("call and response" rhyming competitions between two MC's).[11]

---

[9]   For further discussion, please see Ashahed M. Muhammad, ed., "Hip hop: The Voice of Youth and Social Activism," *FinalCall.Com News,* 07 August 2008 [database-on-line], Accessed March 27, 2009.

[10]   Universal Zulu Nation is an international hip hop awareness group that arose in the 1970's as reformed New York City gang members began to organize cultural events for youth, combining local dance and music movements into what would become known as the various elements of hip hop culture.

[11]   For further discussion on this topic, please see Alan, Light, ed., *The Vibe History of Hip-Hop* (New York: Three Rivers Press, 1999).

Youth from Youth Ministries for Peace and Justice performing in the Bronx.

These performers tend to be the most talked about pioneers of Hip-hop, but I must also include other important figures as well, such as the Latin Empire; a Hip-hop group that consists of Tony Boston (Krazy Taino) and Rick Rodriguez (Puerto Rock), two Puerto Rican cousins from the South Bronx; and the infamous DJ Disco Wiz and MC Prince Whipper Whip, also Puerto Rican of early Hip-hop. Other key players of the hip-hop culture, particularly those from the 1980's generation, include MC LL Cool J, MC Run DMC, Crazy Legs (B-boy), DJ Marley Marl, MC Kurtis Blow, MC Kool and the Gang, MC's Boogie Down Productions, female MC's Salt-N-Peppa and MC's De La Soul.

Over the course of its forty year history, the Hip-hop culture in the South Bronx has facilitated a cross-cultural, cooperative, communicative and spiritual gathering of diverse marginalized youth from all over the city. These public discourses represented for many youth the socio-historical realties of the South Bronx—which was often unknown to those outside its context.

Me at the birthplace of Hip-hop, 1520 Sedgwick Avenue in the Bronx.

In the introduction of their book, *Yes Yes Y'all: The Experience Music Project Oral History of Hip-hop's First Decade,* Jim Fricke and Charlie Ahearn summarize the social conditions in the South Bronx as such:

> "The Bronx, the only one of the five boroughs physically connected to the U.S. mainland, became the symbol of all that allied us. A brief survey of statistics from the southern end of the borough in the 70's tells us a horrific tale. The medium family income in New York was $9,662; in the South Bronx it was $5,200. The area suffered one-quarter of all the city's reported cases of malnutrition. The infant mortality rate was 29 in 1,000 births. There were 6,000 abandoned buildings there. In the pivotal year of 1975, there were 13,000 fires in a twelve-square-mile radius that left more than 10,000 people

homeless and earned landlords $10 million in insurance settlements."[12]

One of Hip-hop's founding fathers, DJ Grandmaster Flash, lived through the above statistics, which compelled him to rhyme about it thereafter. In a song entitled *The Message,* Grandmaster Flash chants:

"Broken glass everywhere/
People pissing on the stairs, you know they just don't care/
I cant take the smell, I cant take the noise/
Got no money to move out, I guess I got no choice/
Rats in the front room, roaches in the back/
Junkies in the alley with a baseball bat/
I tried to get away, but I couldn't get far/
Cause the man with the tow-truck repossessed my car/
Standing on the front stoop, hanging out the window/
Watching all the cars go by, roaring as the breezes blow/"
Don't push me, cause I'm close to the edge/
I'm trying not to loose my head/
It's like a jungle sometimes, it makes me wonder/
How I keep from going under/"[13]

Like so many other MC's of the past and present, DJ Grandmaster Flash can be viewed as the eyes and ears of his own social realities—projected through the lens of the Hip-hop culture. Consequently, DJ Grandmaster Flash used his (words), or MC-ing, in *The Message* in order to convey the:

"Harsh realities of ghetto life, only to put it into a Hip-hop beat. Raw, and full of a passion that only a person who lived what they spoke could have, Flash and his crew explained the depressed environment that they grew up in and the toll it took on the spirit and the minds of the people."[14]

---

[12]   Charlie Ahearn, eds., *Yes Yes Y'all: The Experience Music Project Oral History of Hip-Hop's First Decade* (New York: Da Capo Press, 2002), 2.

[13]   Grandmaster Flash and the Furious Five, *The Message,* The Message, Sugar Hill Records, 1982.

[14]   Tayannah Lee McQuillar and Brother J, *When Rap Music Had a Conscience: The Artists, Organizations and Historic Events that Inspired and Influenced the Golden Age of Hip-Hop from 1987 to 1996* (New York: Thunder's Mouth Press, 2007), 5.

In essence, these MC's became social critics of the injustices that plagued the borough of the Bronx and beyond.

In 1996, criminologist and urban sociologist George Kelling and Catherine Coles released a book entitled, *Fixing Broken Windows: Restoring Order and Reducing Crime in Our Communities*. Both authors reference the "Broken Windows Theory" which states that "fear of crime is strongly related to the existence of disorderly conditions in neighborhoods and communities."[15] In other words, disorder in urban neighborhoods leads to disorderly behavior.

Grandmaster Flash, along with many other Bronx-natives, was already aware of the crime that existed in his neighborhoods because he *lived* there. Therefore, in the eyes of the Hip-hop culture, Grand Master Flash had already assessed and called out the situation by referring to the "Broken Glass Theory" as "Broken Glass Everywhere."

The Broken Glass Theory was defined fourteen years *after* the release of Grandmaster Flashes song *The Message,* which came out in 1982. Unfortunately, DJ Grandmaster Flash's *Message* has been overlooked by people searching for a more aggressive approach. In 1990, New York City Mayor Rudolf Giuliani implemented a "zero tolerance" policy to alleviate future crimes, particularly in the South Bronx.[16] The Broken Glass Theory was used to create a strategic plan that permitted the New York Police Department to have a high police presence in "hot spot" neighborhoods, as well as on-the-scene arrest.

Sadly, the implementation of both theories and legal policies in and around the South Bronx has historically affected marginalized youth communities in ways that has left many of them feeling oppressed and dehumanized. During this period, one of the most destructive tools being used against South Bronx residents was gentrification.

No other person in New York City can attest more thoroughly to the gentrification that had took place in the Bronx than urban planner

---

15 George Kelling and Catherine Coles, *Fixing Broken Windows: Restoring Order and Reducing Crime in Our Communities* (New York: Martin Kessler Books, The Free Press, 1996), 1.

16 For further discussion on this topic, please see *Franklin E. Zimring, The Great American Crime Decline: Studies in Crime and Public Policy (New York: Oxford University Press, 2007).*

Robert Moses. In his book *Can't Stop, Won't Stop: A History of the Hip-Hop Generation,* Jeff Chang talks about Robert Moses' strategic urban planning when he quotes him by stating:

"60,000 Bronx residents were caught in the cross hairs of the expressways [interstate 95, for example]. Moses would bull doze right over them. 'There are more people in the way-that's all,' he would say, as if lives were just another mathematical problem to be solved, there's very little hardship in the thing."[17]

Gentrification, and to some extent urbanization, brought with it a host of other problems, like the displacement example I quoted above. But the bigger problem it brought to South Bronx residents was poverty.

In his book *The Hip-hop Generation: Young Blacks and the Crisis in African-American Culture,* Bakari Kitwana discusses the many common disparities that are found in the Bronx and other urban areas of the United States, particularly amongst African-American communities. Bakari Kitwana indentifies the "Hip-hop generation," as being individuals born between 1965 and 1984 (I was born in 1982). He identifies the common

---

[17]   Chang, 11.

disparity of poverty as being synonymous with the Hip-hop generation. Following the 1970's and 1980's, Bakari Kitwana goes on to say the following regarding this generational trend of poverty among urban Black youth:

"According to the U.S. Consensus Bureau, in 1999, the number of Blacks living below the poverty line had dropped to its lowest level in nearly three decades, many young Blacks remain poor and working poor. The Urban Institute estimates that 60 percent of America's poor youth are Black."[18]

With high levels of poverty, especially amongst poor young Blacks and other minority groups, high rates of crime became prevalent, particularly, when it came to drug consumption and distribution.

Beginning in the early 1980's, the Reagan administration fought rigorously to suppress drugs in the United States. Former President Ronald Reagan implemented a "War on Drugs" strategy that discontinued countless rehabilitative programs, particularly in the urban sector. In turn, thousands of young men, mostly Black and Latino, were convicted under the mandatory minimum sentencing scheme, which left them imprisoned for exaggerated periods of time.[19] Bakari Kitwana further adds to this when he references the disproportionate sentences of crack cocaine violations between Whites and Blacks. He states the following:

"The National Institute on drug abuse has indicated that by 1990, most crack cocaine users were White. Yet, in the early 1990's, 90 percent of those convicted in federal court of crack cocaine crimes were Black."[20]

This desire to have harsher punishments for drug involvement also had an effect on how police conducted themselves toward minority urban youth living in the South Bronx.

---

[18] Bakari Kitwana, *The Hip-hop Generation: Young Blacks and the Crisis in African-American Culture* (New York: The Perseus Books Group, 2002), 20.

[19] For further discussion on this topic, please see Doris Provine, *Unequal under Law: Race in the War on Drugs* (Chicago: University of Chicago Press, 2007).

[20] Kitwana, 14.

Me speaking to community activists in Colombia, South America.

In her book *Street Justice: A History of Police Violence in New York City,* strategist and professor of history Marilynn S. Johnson talks about the cycles of police brutality and reform in New York City.

"Constrained by new laws and regulations, police [specifically the New York City Police Department] have found ways to conceal or justify misconduct. As a student in a federal law enforcement training program, in the 1980's, I was struck by the amount of time and energy invested in teaching the proper 'articulation' of probable cause, reasonable suspicion, and the use of deadly force—suggesting the objective circumstances of a police action could be reconstructed to fit legal requirements."[21]

Law enforcement training instructors who teach justifying misconduct is the reason why Bakari Kitwana stated that "in New York City, complaints of police brutality rose nearly fifty percent in 1994 alone."[22] According to Marilynn S Johnson, percentages such as the one that Bakari has given do in fact represent the history of New York City police misconduct; to some extent, even today (most recently, was the Sean Bell incident where he was shot 50 times and neither of the police officer's that were involved

---

[21] Marilynn S. Johnson, *Justice: A History of Police Violence in New York City* (Boston: Beacon Press, 2004), 2.

[22] Kitwana,, 17.

were indicted). Needless to say, when we look at Bakari Kitwana's fifty percent figure from the standpoint of the South Bronx alone, the numbers become even more staggering.

An MC from Queens named Nas rhymed about police misconduct and social abuse in a song entitled *Middle Finger*. Nas, born in the 1970's, is a product of this intergenerational police abuse and he states the following:

"Now all you hypocrites, witness the injustice/
Conversations taped illegally, then they cuff us/
U.S. attorneys, public defenders send us off to hard prison time/
Whether you innocent or did the crime/
Say you come from? Pursue your heart/
Run your place, put guns in your face/
Put you in the cuffs for nothing/
Now your struggling, tied up, standing in line-ups/
Call your lawyer, they charged you with murder/
Why? Cuz these liars said you shot another man on his driveway/
Guilty, just for being Black on a Friday/
Polygraph test your feelings, because your nervous/
Charged for murder you didn't commit, then they serve ya/
Fifteen years, maximum security/
Slashing, stab wounds, broken bone injuries/
You were placed there intentionally/
Either you bang or you miss me, listen to me/"[23]

Nas describes his frustration with law enforcement as result of their ongoing distrust of African-Americans (and vise versa). The same critique that Nas gives of police misconduct can also be applied to the disproportionate number of minorities that were being incarcerated during the maturation years of Hip-hop culture.

Regrettably, today, the process is different. This time, we are seeing it happening in places where we least expect them; I shall explain. Many minority youth in the Bronx have grown up fearing, distrusting and

---

[23]   Nas, *Middle Finger,* Untitled, Def Jam and Columbia Records, 2008.

disliking the police. This is partially due to the fact that the public school systems in the Bronx have always supported a high police presence in and around school grounds. This in turn creates a prison-like atmosphere for these youth, which in the long run becomes a self-fulfilling prophecy—incarceration.

The 6 train to the Bronx.

Nora Sam Ahmed and Jose Sanchez both talk about their experiences as public school teachers in the South Bronx. They say the following about this pre-incarceration environment:

"The callous disregard for human life is a daily happening in our inner city schools. The reality of metal detectors, abusive police and the systemic stigmatization of children of color as criminals in schools are conveniently hidden behind stories of achievements of our educational systems."[24]

This intimidation of minority youth by police in the public schools of the Bronx is one of the reasons why "the Bureaus of Justice have approximately fifty percent federal and state prisoners being people of African-American descent."[25] Additionally, the risk of getting thrown in prison by the police is as high as the health risk that continues to impair Bronx residents.

The South Bronx is notorious for not only being one of the poorest districts in the United States; it also has one of the highest asthma rates in the country. The latter of these two deplorable realities has a lot to due with none other than New York City's infamous urban planner, Robert Moses. His plans included building multiple highways in and around the South Bronx section of the city [26] and with every expressway and byway that was built traffic from commercial eighteen wheelers increased. These trucks spewed out excessive amounts of air pollutants triggering a high rate of acute asthma among many youth in the South Bronx.[27]

And so, for many youth growing up in this period (1980's and 1990's) of time, the possibility of hope and change became more unrealistic because of higher incarceration rates, rising poverty, harsh laws, displacement and health concerns in the Bronx; especially taking into consideration the "great disparities in education, housing, health care, employment opportunities, wages and mortgage loan approvals."[28]

The above statistics, policies, theories and city development are only a few examples of the sociological realities and historical facts that helped shape the Hip-hop culture. The Hip-hop community and its culture

---

[24]   Nora Sam Ahmed and Jose Sanchez, ed., *From Bronx High School Teachers* [database-on-line]; available from http://www.worldcantwait.net; Internet; accessed 8 December 2008.

[25]   Kitwana, 53.

[26]   For further discussion on this topic, please see Robert Caro, *The Power Broker: Robert Moses and the Fall of New York* (New York: Vintage Books, 1974).

[27]   For further discussion on this topic, please see Martha Brenner, *Emergency Asthma: Clinical Allergy and Immunology* (New York: *Marcel dramatist Ltd*, 1999).

[28]   Kitwana,10.

continue to put a spotlight on the injustices that plague New York City and other U.S. cities—most notably through its diverse voices.

After emigrating from Peru, Felipe Coronel, who goes by the MC name Immortal Technique, settled into the Harlem section of New York City where he became a witness to these disparities first hand. In a song entitled *Modern Day Slavery*, he, along with MC Joel Ortiz, poured out his soul in reaction to these injustices, which to him resemble a form of modern day slavery.

> "Our people are the product of genocide and slavery/
> Everything in the ghetto was how it was made to be/
> Designed in a process, Prison Industrial Complex/
> Nigg*z transformed into numbers and objects/
> We pay the devil rent for living in hell/
> Cuz the projects was built on the spot where Lucifer fell/
> Incarcerated knowledge and heavy weight/
> Every Black man should read Deuteronomy Chapter 28/
> Cursed in the city like we're cursed in the field/
> Cursed on the border, and cursed by the New World Order/
> Our sons and daughters were stolen by another people/
> Gentrifying the earth, land of the eagle/
> This is the sequel to the prophecy/
> Freedom when peaceful then violent is my philosophy/
> I built an army, now I'm gonna build a nation/
> The foundation of a new civilization/
> And overthrow the plantation/"[29]

This was the world that was confronted by Immortal Technique. Hip-hop culture became for him the vessel through which he appealed to his audience to take notice of and resist the injustices that were affecting him as an individual and as a member of a much broader social reality.

DJ Kool Herc, DJ Grandmaster Flash, Porto Rock and Run DMC and many others, made this public discourse available for marginalized youth when they allowed those unspoken voices to finally express themselves in a public setting regarding the systems—school, criminal justice and

---

[29]   Joel Ortiz, *Modern Day Slavery*, The Brick: Bodega Chronicles, Koch Records, 2007.

government—that were destroying them as a community. For many youth in the South Bronx, what appeared to be nothing more than a life of struggle, pain, and loss was being substituted by words of hope, inspiration, joy and most importantly, feelings of being a spiritual being.

Me chilling with DJ Nocturnal.

Earlier in my introduction I stated that Hip-hop resembles a church, particularly a church from the First Century. This includes having the same spirit as that which brought followers of Jesus Christ together, as seen in the many faces and heard in the many voices that helped bring people together in the South Bronx. In other words, the parallelism that is found between these two time periods can be seen in various (synthetic) levels; I shall explain.

In antiquity, many of the same harsh socio-historical realities that faced the first "Christians" (as they were building their churches) can be seen in the experiences of diverse marginalized youth in the South Bronx during the outset of Hip-hop's culture. For example, in addition to the ramifications of urban planning that I have mentioned earlier, such as poverty, police misconduct and health risks, the residents of the South Bronx also had to deal with seeing their neighborhood go up in flames, literally.

Jeff Chang describes the reason for these fires in more detail:

"Apartment buildings passed into the hands of slumlords, who soon figured out that they could make more money by refusing to provide heat and water to the tenants, withholding property taxes from the city, and finally destroying the building [by burning it] for insurance money."[30]

These fires, symbolically speaking, resembled the Great Fires of Rome (64 Common Era) which resulted in the persecution of countless "Christians" (Christians is in quotations because the first followers of Jesus Christ weren't called that at first; they were called followers of "The Way") throughout the Roman Empire.[31] It was during this time that many of the first "Christians" were abused, tortured and murdered by the Roman Empire and its soldiers. Similarly, many South Bronx residents have been the victims of countless abuses and dislocations as a result of the "empire," the United States, and its "soldiers," the New York Police Department.

At first, it may have appeared that these harsh conditions would eventually destroy these communities. However, history has shown us that both Hip-hop culture and Christianity have in fact planted the seeds for the *transformation* of their own communities and the world. Over the course of this historical transformation, Christianity has evolved and created churches that symbolize Jesus' attempt to bring heaven a little closer to earth. In the same way, Hip-hop culture (over the course of its history) has tried to build its own churches and communities, by attempting to bring "God's House" a little closer to its children in the streets.

I am a firm believer that Hip-hop has a place within the Christian mission of doing ministerial work, having the church present in peoples' lives (in and out of its four walls) and in social justice. Hip-hop carries with it the same spiritual conviction(s) that were present in the lives and social conditions of those suffering [minority] Christians in ancient Rome; only this time, it is the [minority] youth in the Bronx—who suffer discrimination and poor social conditions.

---

[30] Chang, 13.

[31] For further discussion on this topic, please see H.D.M. Spencer-Jones, *The Early Christians in Rome,* 2nd ed. (London: Metheun, 1911).

Based on the above socio-historical analysis of Hip-hop culture, we can see that the spirit that eventually compelled Christians to grow beyond their suffering in the Roman Empire is the same spirit that drives these youth of the Hip-hop culture to speak out and take action in the United States. This is indicative of the power of the Holy Spirit, which shows up in unpredictable places.

To claim through this socio-historical analysis that Hip-hop culture is spiritual requires that we first look at what it means to be spiritual. In other words, what does a spiritual experience look or feel?

CHAPTER 2:

In the Spirit of Hip-Hop

The spirit of my family is upon me because their example has taught me to care deeply for other people. And to work in collaboration with others to fight injustices and to build communities.

—Anonymous

Music is also theological. That is, it tells us about the Divine Spirit that moves the people toward unity and self-determination.

—Dr. James Cone

Charles A. Briggs Distinguished Professor of Systematic Theology at Union Theological Seminary

"The Spirit of God lives in us."

—Eminem

From the song entitled *'Till I Collapse*

It was the summer of 2006 and I had accompanied my cousins and their friends to see our favorite Hip-hop group of all time—The Wu-Tang Clan. They were on a national tour to mourn the loss of one of their original and most important members, the Ol' Dirty Bastard. The loss was the reason why this tour was so special for the self-described "Wu-Heads," or Wu-tang Clan fanatics; it also explains why this particular concert was sold out within its first week of ticket sales.

I remember at one point during the concert, stopping for a brief moment to observe the great ocean of people that were in attendance that evening. One of the many things I reflected upon was the diversity of people present, varying in race, age, socioeconomic status, sexual orientation—all kinds of people.

But what I remember most was watching the crowd moving as a group, almost exactly in sync, their whole bodies to the same beats and words that were being orated by these MC's. It was at that same exact moment, everyone, including myself, was repeating exactly what the opening MC, Inspectah Deck, espoused:

"I bomb atomically, Socrates' philosophies and hypothesis/
Can't define how I be dropping these/
Mockeries/
Lyrically perform armed robbery/
Flee with the lottery/
Possibly they spotted me/
Battle-scarred shogun, explosion when my pen hits/
Tremendous, ultra-violet shine blind forensics/
I inspect you, through the future see millennium/
Killa B's sold fifty gold sixty platinum/
Shackling the masses with drastic rap tactics/
Graphic displays melt the steel like blacksmiths/
Black Wu jackets queen B's ease the guns in/
Rumble with patrolmen, tear gas laced the function/
Heads by the score take flight incite a war/
Chicks hit the floor, diehard fans demand more/
Behold the bold soldier, control the globe slowly/
Proceeds to blow swinging swords like Shinobi/
Stomp grounds and pound footprints in solid rock/
Wu got it locked, performing live on your hottest block/"[32]

It was at that very moment where I felt a personal connection with both the audience and the MC. It was impossible not to gravitate toward this contagious instrumentation with raw lyrics. As we, the audience and the MC's, moved our bodies to the same beat and motion, I could not help but feel a greater spiritual connection the more I listened to these words as they were both intellectually stimulating and emotionally gratifying.

---

[32]   Wu-Tang Clan, *Triumph,* Wu-Tang Forever, Loud/RCA/BMG Records, 1997.

Me with a community organizer in Mississippi.

What I felt that night—stimulation of both the mind and the body—reminded me of the form of worship that can be seen in one particular Christian denomination, Pentecostalism. With the focus of God and using the gifts of the Holy Spirit as worship, the Pentecostal experience is almost identical to how youth in the Hip-hop culture express and experience God's spirit in the hood. This will be discussed in greater detail moving forward.

Nevertheless, trying to articulate what I experienced that night at the concert would be extremely challenging without providing the proper context. More specifically, does Hip-hop create or provide spiritual experiences for youth? And most importantly, how does spirituality present itself in every day social settings?

Professor Roger Haight, a Scholar in Residence at Union Theological Seminary in New York City, once said in his class, *Spirituality, Ethics and Theology*, that, "spirituality is the way persons or *groups* lead their lives *in light of their relation to ultimate reality.*" Similarly, Professor Gustavo Gutiérrez in his book, *A Theology of Liberation*, defined spirituality as "a way of *being* Christian.*"[33] In other words, both professors agree that

---

[33] Gustavo Gutiérrez, *A Theology of Liberation* (New York: Orbis Books, 1988), 32.

spirituality can be experienced beyond the confinements of the church *and* the privacy of ones' own home (the safest place in an unsafe world). It also can be experienced collectively, including outside of the church and into society.

The difficulty with having a collective spirituality is that our society is always changing. But when we talk about the role of spirituality *within* history, we are referring to the *same* spirit that has been helping to draw people toward a deeper relationship with God, for years.

The encounters between people and their social circumstances is where we encounter God, or spirituality, around us—not necessarily from a top-down approach, but with a conscientious awareness of varying situations and circumstances. This view on spirituality explains the need for a more socio-historical perspective of Hip-hop in the preceding chapter, as it was from this place and space in the South Bronx where we see a spirit that manifests itself from the people and "catches" the attention of God by drawing Him near to them.

Me and my classmates getting ready to perform for a chapel service at the 2008 Hispanic Summer Program in Chicago, Illinois.

In his book *Go and Do Likewise: Jesus and Ethics*, William Spohn describes for us the experience of God into two terms: The Dialectical

Imagination and The Analogical Imagination. The latter discourse "begins with experiences of the manifestation of God's graciousness in ordinary life and moves from that to try to understand God." The Dialectical Imagination, on the other hand, is the "empowering experience of God's decisive word of address in Jesus Christ."[34]

Because Dialectical Imagination brings with it an "empowering experience of God," a relationship is established between the individual(s) and God because of this personal spiritual connection that is "felt," or experienced (which in some cases, may come to the individual when he or she is reading the Bible or praying in church, for example). Hence, the Dialectical Imagination is something that comes to us from "above," which later inspires us to do something "below"—so it is viewed as being vertical.

In the case of the Analogical Imagination, the discourse comes to the person from "below" because it manifests itself "in ordinary life" situations and circumstances. Consequently, day-to-day encounters with people in our society become just as important to the spiritual seeker as reading the Bible or participating in church, especially when it comes to "experiencing" God. Unlike the Dialectical Imaginations, the Analogical Imagination, in essence, is horizontal because it starts from "below" and then spreads outwards throughout the earth.

So when we talk about Hip-hop being spiritual, I am looking at it from the vantage point of view of the Analogical Imagination. In other words, when the community gathers together in the name of Hip-hop, it can be viewed as another way that marginalized youth "experience the manifestation of God's graciousness in their ordinary life"—this in turn inspires them to try to understand how God's influence is present in their own personal lives and social realities.

The previous chapter listed several of the harsh conditions that many of the youth faced while living in the South Bronx, including but not limited to: police misconduct, poverty and gentrification. These were, and in some respects, continue to be, the realities that are still faced by many marginalized youth in the South Bronx—and other urban cities—today.

When MC's or graffiti artists express these realities using the Hip-hop culture, they in turn create a space that freely invites people into an emotional and invigorating space.

---

34   William Spohn, *Go and Do Likewise: Jesus and Ethics* (New York: Continuum International Publishing Group, 1999), 60.

I believe that this spiritual connection becomes more intensified in the public places of the world as opposed to the domesticated and exclusiveness of a spirit that is trapped indoors (i.e. church). Being out in the public's eye; however, suggests that the spirit is more inclusive. It also demonstrates to those around it that a collective emotion is more powerful because it allows *all* types of people from the community to come together, especially "the least of these" (Matthew 25: 40),[35] and makes them one.

One of the best known MC's for projecting his spiritual emotions vividly is Earl Simmons, better known as DMX. In his song entitled, *The Convo,* DMX holds an emotional conversation with God about his struggle and survival in the streets. He says the following:

"You tell me that there's love here, but to me it's blatant/
Nothing but all the blood here, I'm dealing with Satan/
Plus with all the hating, it's hard to keep peace/
Thou shall not steal, but I will to eat/
I tried doing good, but good's not too good for me/
Misunderstood, why you chose the hood for me/
Mean I'm alright, I just had to work hard at it/
Went to grandma for answers, she told me that God had it/
So now here I am, confused and full of questions/
Am I born to lose, or is this just a lesson/
And who is it going to choose when it gets turned around?/
And will it be laying in my own blood and on the ground?/"[36]

DMX's outcry to God in his life exemplifies the many youth I have worked with who struggle to make sense of their conditions. And so, it becomes fitting that emotion stirs up whenever we vent on these social realities.

Emotion, which is so difficult to put into words, is something that is associated a lot with spirituality. This is why in the beginning of this chapter, a correlation between spirituality and the concepts of feeling and emotion is made. That is not to say that spirituality is something that

---

[35] The New Oxford Annotated Bible, Revised Standard Version, (New York: Oxford University Press, 1973).

[36] DMX, *The Convo,* It's Dark and Hell is Hot, Def Jam/Ruff Ryders Records, 1998.

cannot be experienced on an intellectual level. On the contrary, it works just as much on a cognitive level as it does on a bodily/physical level.

Hip-hop culture has, and always will be, no stranger to emotion. But for the purposes of this discussion, I will focus mainly on the emotion that comes from the MC—because as a spoken word and MC artist of the Hip-hop culture, I have insight into this element of Hip-hop.

Me and the founder of the Latino Pastoral Action Center in the Bronx, Reverend Doctor Raymond Rivera.

Emotion is something that has always characterized an authentic MC [37] because emotion brings to the audience a heart-felt need, or concern, to do something (as opposed to just saying something). In his book *Spirituality and Human Emotion,* Robert C. Roberts argues that emotion is founded upon none other than a *concern*. In other words, Robert's believes that:

---

[37] An Authentic MC is someone who rhymes from the heart as well as from his/her knowledge and wisdom. He/she speaks about those same social conditions that are affecting them personally in order to change the broader society. He/she is original in their lyrics, and, uses emotion to insight consciousness and human agency. All in all, an authentic MC uses his/her words to build communities of hope, love, justice and peace.

"The capacity to be affected emotionally is not only a characteristic of weak people but also of very strong ones. Churchill, Socrates, and the Apostle Paul were all strong people of deep feeling. It is in fact, among other things, that they are 'driven' by some passion or other—whether it be love of country, concern for intellectual and moral integrity, or the love of God—that makes concerned people such strong, integrated persons. But their passion is also the basis for a wide repertoire of emotions."[38]

As a Christian, I have heard many other Christians complement each other by saying: "That person has the Holy Spirit in them." This statement is acknowledging the fact that that particular person's emotion is helping him or her to communicate God's message. This understanding of the Spirit as being emotional is common among Christian believers, most notably, I believe, amongst our Pentecostal brothers and sisters. Inspired by the Day of Pentecost in the Book of Acts in the New Testament, the Holy Spirit is something that Pentecostal believers believe can be experienced by anyone. As a Roman Catholic, however, I am aware that the Spirit is very much important and alive in other Christian denominations (and religions) as well.

Spirituality and emotion is something that many congregants in the Pentecostal tradition experience while worshiping. I myself have experienced this emotion numerous times, only it manifests itself when I am performing my spoken word pieces.

In a Pentecostal service, the pastor, or in some cases, the congregants, preaches or sings in an "extraordinary" way as a result of being infused and guided by the Holy Spirit. This spiritual experience, according to Pentecostals, is interpreted as having a "direct" connection with God. An MC who expresses words of struggle and pain to the audience can also bring with it a level of emotion that can connect him or her to God—this is not meant to devalue the lyrical skills of the MC, which can be seen as being a gift *by* the Holy Spirit.

Spiritual gifts are something that characterizes Pentecostalism, such as being "enwrapped" in the Holy Spirit. Gifts are supposed to demonstrate

---

[38] Robert C. Roberts, *Spirituality and Human Emotion* (Grand Rapids, Michigan: William B. Eerdmans Publishing Company, 1982), 14.

to the non-believers that God *is* working in their lives. This spiritual gift is the same spiritual force that describes the experience that is sometimes felt during these Hip-hop sessions, which probably explains why it too draws non-believers into its realm.

In the chapters that follow, I will discuss in more depth the relationship that is visible between Pentecostal churches and Hip-hop shows (which will also help to explain why, according to my research, Pentecostal churches are known to embrace the culture of Hip-hop more than any other Christian denomination). But as I mentioned previously, spirituality is an experience that can also be felt on a subconscious level, as opposed to just being fervent. In his book entitled, *Spirituality and Moral Theology: Essays from a Pastoral Perspective,* James Keating attempts to make a connection between spiritual life and moral life by demonstrating how spirituality is important to the formation of consciousness. He goes on to say the following about consciousness:

> "Consciousness is a deep and abiding hunger within us to move beyond ourselves, a moral appetite constantly urging us beyond all our limits and boundaries, calling us to stretch ourselves beyond our selfish and petty concerns, reaching out for others, the moral good and ultimately for God."[39]

Consciousness in Hip-hop music has, and always will be, a vital component—as most "Hip-hop heads" would agree. Beginning in the summer of 2008 and ending in March of 2009, I distributed 400 surveys on Hip-hop to people from all over the world.[40] Most of the surveys I distributed came from the various places I have traveled to as part of my research for my Masters of Arts Thesis at Union Theological Seminary

---

[39] James Keating, ed., *Spirituality and Moral Theology: Essays from a Pastoral Perspective* (New York: Paulist Press, 2000), 65.

[40] Throughout my thesis, I will sway back and fourth from the particular (i.e. the South Bronx and my personal experiences) to the broader (i.e. the world outside of the United States context). The latter perspective will be mentioned briefly in the subsequent chapters. It is in the conclusion, however, where I will spend most of my time "unwrapping" this broader view on hip-hop; specifically my experience at Colombia in South America. This will demonstrate how hip-hop is—also—impacting the global community.

in New York City. I sent these anonymous surveys out to a wide range of audiences: youth, elderly, professionals, college students, clergy, high school students, Black, White, Latino/a, Asians, Jews, Muslims, male, female, gay, lesbian, atheist, North Americans, Colombians, Swiss, Dutch, married and single folks. The survey asked a series of brief questions on topics that I will—or already have—touched on, such as spirituality, youth outreach, and Hip-hop's global implications.

One of the most interesting pieces of information that I received from the 100 (out of 400) surveys that were returned back to me indicated that an overwhelming majority, 96%, believed that Hip-hop is neither dead nor obsolete. In fact, most people believed that Hip-hop is just going through a "phase of recession." Posing such a question helped me verify that although many people view Hip-hop as "not what it used to be," it still is part of their lives. Actually, most people in the surveys stated that Hip-hop is diversifying and growing in those very same places that I am referring to in my thesis: church, academia, social activism, spoken word and youth ministry programs.

But getting back to the conscious element of Hip-hop; another (relevant) question that I posed asked the following: What characteristics make up a good MC? Not surprisingly, an overwhelming majority agreed that some level of consciousness or knowledge was necessary in order to catch their personal attention. In other words, the content of the music is just as important as its beats,[41] or for that matter, its volume in sales.

For many, myself included, it is the words that make up a song, especially when they are words that call us to challenge our own moral agency. Therefore, this kind of self-reflection by way of self-expression, or Hip-hop, can also be looked upon as another way we can develop a more intimate relationship with God. James Keating further adds to this by stating that:

"To hear the call of conscious is to be aware of the divine intervention to become more fully and authentically human.

---

[41] A Beat is either live (non-rehearsed) or produced (pre-rehearsed), with a clearly defined drum beat (almost always in 4/4 time signature); which is presented either with or without vocal accompaniment. In other words, there are 4 beats to every rhyme verse, and in every rhyme verse there are 4 sentences. All of the words at the end of each sentence must sound like the word that preceded it. This pattern get repeated over and over again; depending how long the song is.

At one level, conscious, is the call to be an imitator of Christ, since it is Jesus alone who has plumbed the depths of what it means to be human."[42]

To hear "the call of conscious," as James Keating puts it, is exactly the factor that appeals to many youth when we talk about Hip-hop music. Critiquing our own moral judgments, and in most cases, the moral integrity of the various institutions that exists (i.e. institutionalized religion and government), *is* what many great MC's are composed of.

One example of this conscious building comes from a well known MC who goes by the name of Common. In a song entitled, *G.O.D. (Gaining One's Definition)*, Common rhymes about religious open-mindedness and spirituality, while critiquing the religious (institutional) abuse that comes with not posing any spiritual questions and challenges. He goes on to say the following:

"In time brotha, you will discover the light/
Some say that God is Black and the Devil's White/
Well, the Devil is wrong and God is what's right/
I fight, with myself in the ring of doubt and fear /
The rain ain't gone, but I can still see clear/
As a child, given religion with no answers to why/
Just told believe in Jesus because for me he did die/
Curiosity killed the catechism/
Understanding and wisdom became the rhythm that I played to/
And became a slave to master self /
A rich man is one with knowledge, happiness and his health/
My mind had dealt with the books of Zen, Tao the lessons/
Koran and the Bible, to me they all vital/
And got truth within them, gotta read them boys/
You just can't skim them, different branches of belief/
But one root that stem them, but people of the venom try to trim them/
And use religion as an emblem/
When it should be a natural way of life/

---

42   Keating, 65.

Who am I or they to say to whom you pray ain't right/
That's who got you doing right and got you this far/
Whether you say "in Jesus name" or "Hum do Allah"/
Long as you know it's a being that's supreme to you/
You let that show towards others in the things you do/"[43]

Combining emotion with intellect, or consciousness, is what helps to capture this spiritual space that Hip-hop helps to create for marginalized youth. It almost seems that with every word that is said and with every emotion that is felt, the MC continues to draw youth into his or her spiritual realm and consciousness.

Consequently, what you get over time, in some instances, is a Hip-hop whose spirituality can be viewed as being more "holistic" because it creates a larger spiritual experience as a result of people gravitating to its messages.

If this is the case, then we must ask ourselves the following questions: Does this spiritual setting, which occurs on occasion, make us rethink about the secular as being something that is actually sacred? If the answer is yes, than can Hip-hop be utilized as a way of *worshiping* God? These are only a few of the many questions that I will try to answer in the next chapter.

---

[43]   Common, *G.O.D. (Gaining One's Definition),* One Day It'll All Make Sense, Relativity Records, 1997.

CHAPTER 3:

Worshipping to the Beat of Hip-hop

"For me, music is a great way to connect with people that you might not have other means to connect with, actually. You may not speak the same language, you may not come from the same culture, but you can share a song, you can share a moment of a musical experience in a really profound way. And the capacity of music to be communicative in that respect is unlike any other art form . . . A dialogue through the audio and the visual."

—Sharif Ezzat a.k.a. Witness

Differing musical styles allows people of differing backgrounds, ages and experiences to worship God wholeheartedly together.
—Bob Kauflin

I rip shows, stay focused, and split cheese, with soldiers/
While you hit trees and coast I spit flows that be ferocious/
And with these explosives, I split seas for Moses/
Shine permanently only my mind's concerning me/
Fire burns in me eternally time's eternity/
Followers turn on me they'll be in a mental infirmary/
Determinedly advance technology better than Germany/
Since the first days you know of, 'till the last days is over/
I was always the flow-er, I made waves for Noah/

—Rakim
From the song entitled The 18th Letter

In the fall of 2008, I was invited by Professor Janet Walton, a Professor of Worship at Union Theological Seminary, to lecture on Hip-hop for her Introduction to Preaching and Worship class. About a week before that lecture had taken place, Professor Janet and I came together to discuss the layout of the lecture. At one point during our discussion, I remember asking her the following question: What does worship mean to you? She looked up at me and said, "Worship is about honoring those that are there, and those that are not, or have been excluded."

I was somewhat surprised at Professor Walton's response, as I was anticipating a more academically constructed response to my question. Instead, I felt like she gave me an answer that was honest and real. Because of her response, I came out of that meeting understanding why she had asked me to talk about Hip-hop culture in her class—up until that point, Hip-hop culture had been excluded . . . . from worship!

Me and more graffiti art work in Geneva, Switzerland.

A few days after my meeting with Professor Janet Walton, I went to the South Bronx to attend Holy Hood's service at the Latino Pastoral Action Center (LPAC). [44] As was the case on every Friday night, youth from all over New York City (about 50 total) gathered around to praise and worship—Jesus Christ—inside a room endorsed with graffiti art work on the wall mixed with several excerpts from the Christian Bible.

Before the service began, promptly at 7:00 P.M., everyone gathered around this table for a brief agape meal. When that was completed, everyone sat down in their own seat to hear the Rev. Raymond Rivera, the founder of LPAC, speak. I remember the first thing he said to us:

---

[44] Founded in 1992 by Reverend Raymond Rivera, the New York City based Latino Pastoral Action Center (LPAC) is a national faith-based organization that aims to educate, equip and empower Latino/a and other urban churches to develop holistic ministries.

"Welcome everyone, to God's House. Enjoy your time here, because I know you will. Let's embrace this moment to listen to what God's children have to say to us . . . ." Following Raymond Rivera's statement was a host of performances by various youth; some of these performances included rhyming on stage and break dancing. For me, one of the most powerful segments of this service was the individual public testimonies spoken by the group. Most of the testimonies were delivered to the audience using the spoken word while others used beats to buttress their rhymes.

Members of the Search and Rescue ministry prepping to rhyme and dance for the youth in the Chad Brown Projects in Providence, Rhode Island.

Regardless of the delivery, all of the public testimonies that night detailed real life scenarios of what it's like growing up in and around gang violence and poverty. At the very same time, these testimonies spoke of many words that not only appeared to praise Jesus Christ, but also garner enough merit to be considered as worship.

This worship service was supervised by the youth pastor and youth mentor of Holy Hood, but it was conducted entirely by the participants; this included prayer, worship and the liturgy. In the previous chapter, I mentioned how Pentecostal's Holy Spirit experience resembles the spiritual feeling that is experienced when engaging in the Hip-hop culture.

Here, we are seeing more concrete examples of how youth at Holy Hood utilize public testimonies through Hip-hop as a form of doing Pentecostal worship. This should come as no surprise; Rev. Raymond Rivera is himself a Pentecostal pastor who emphasizes the traditions of Pentecostalism: biblical studies, the recognition of spiritual gifts and worship.

Before delving into the correlation between Pentecostalism and Hip-hop, it is important to have a more complete understanding of what it means to "do" worship. In his book, *Putting an End to Worship Wars,* Elmer Towns defines worship as:

> "A face-to-face encounter with the living God is based on a regeneration experience, prompted by the Holy Spirit, and resulting in the exaltation of God's glory. Simply speaking, worship is giving the 'worth-ship' to God that He deserves because He is God. Therefore, worship should be an emotional, intellectual and volitional response to God."[45]

The biggest argument that Elmer Towns makes in his book is that there exists no one particular methodology of practicing worship, period. In other words, worship is as diverse as the various cultures and ethnicities that distinguish us from one another.

When I refer back to Professor Janet Walton's interpretation of worship, and relate that to Elmer Towns view on the topic, I can help but agree with the notion that Hip-hop, as a culture within itself, can be used as a way of "doing" worship (I put doing in quotations because I believe that worship has been done in so many different ways throughout the course of our history that there is no one way of doing worship, let alone define it).

For example, the Hip-hop Church of Harlem,[46] which gains its support from the AME (African Methodist Episcopal) Church, emphasizes

---

45 Elmer Townes, *Putting an End to Worship Wars* (Tennessee: Broadman & Holman, 1997), 24.

46 The Hip-hop Church of Harlem's mission is to present the Christian gospel in a setting that appeals to both those individuals who are confessed Christians as well as those who are considered un-churched. The Hip Hop Church is worship and scriptural study. It serves to outreach to the disenfranchised, the broken hearted, the oppressed and those considered "disposable" by the larger society. Their worship services follow an order of service consistent with many African-American churches, while always allowing the Holy Spirit to have full reign. Their motto is: "Hip Hop is the culture, while Jesus is the Center."

Scripture reading as part of its worship service. Holy Hood in LPAC also focuses on its Bible readings as part of its worship, but not as frequently as the Hip-hop Church of Harlem. The difference is Holy Hood tends to focus itself more on public testimonies that arise from its congregants through Hip-hop performances; conversely, the Hip-hop Church of Harlem focuses more on the testimonies of its preacher MC's.

Last year, I attended a service at the Hip-hop Church of Harlem, which was started by a man who goes by the name of Kurtis Blow (a DJ and MC from Harlem, New York). To my surprise, their worship began with a teenager reading the scripture for the day, through the ultimate medium of Hip-hop, MC-ing. What would follow is a half-hour live DJ performance in collaboration with a group of students who would take turns rhyming and break dancing. This would happen for about thirty minutes. Following that, the preacher for that evening would give a sermon based on the Biblical text that initiated the ceremony. Finally, it would conclude with a prayer; which, not surprisingly, was orated in a rhyming fashion as well.

Me adjacent to graffiti art work in Geneva, Switzerland.

After the service was over, I left feeling like most of the youth who were present that night—spiritually fulfilled. But on a more personal level, I departed feeling like they could worship God through a forum that was more familiar to them—and to me: Hip-hop.

In previous chapters, I talked about how Hip-hop can be viewed as being a church. In this respect, church can be viewed in two ways. The first is Hip-hop being utilized in a traditional sense; meaning it has all the components that make up what many agree is what defines the church—a pastor, an ornate meeting space, dogma and doctrines. One Hip-hop church that meets these prerequisites is the aforementioned Hip-hop Church of Harlem. The second kind of Hip-hop church is more informal, open to interpretation and not as aesthetically pleasing to the eye—both on the inside and outside. I say that because these types of churches are typically, not always, located in places like office buildings, garages or in some cases, abandoned factories. An example of this is LPAC's Holy Hood.

Holy Hood is situated inside of LPAC's not-for-profit establishment, which includes a basketball court and a charter school. It has no Christian symbols, no altar and no dress code. And even though it preserves its Pentecostal traditions, it does not have a formal creed, doctrine or manual that guides the service. However, what it does have makes us rethink and re-imagine not only what the church looks like, but what its overall function is here on earth. This will be discussed in greater detail as we move forward.

But for right now, it's important to realize how the latter version (Holy Hood) of what it means to be the church, including its style of worship, makes us re-think God's influence on Hip-hop. In other words, Hip-hop's ability to bring a diversity of marginalized youth together in this/a space *is* church. But not just any church, but a church that goes beyond the confinements of its four walls and into the streets. And no matter what the place of worship looks like, who is invited, and how they are invited, God becomes ever so present amongst and within these marginalized people.

A telling example of such activity took place in May of 2007. I attended a Hip-hop block party in the South Bronx that was sponsored by an organization called Critical Resistance.[47] Most of the performers in

---

[47] Critical Resistance is a national grassroots not-for-profit organization committed to ending society's use of prisons and policing as an answer to social problems.

attendance were local MC's that embraced this moment to express their frustration and concerns revolving around the prison system and police interactions.

On that day, I decided to participate in their Open Mic segment. And as a spoken word artist, I—like most of the MC's who rhymed on that day—was able to create a reciprocal emotion through the forum of Hip-hop's worship-style, specifically regarding public testimonies. It is during this moment where one can lose sight of their surroundings. I remember one particular MC who rhymed about how years in prison had changed his life. This MC delivered to the audience, and to himself, a deep sense of emotion, some of which included words of joy and sadness, accompanied with an occasional tear, and followed by silence.

The Hip-hop Church of Harlem.

Like other similar events that I have participated in, the kind of emotion experienced at this event is the reason why I see a similar connection between Hip-hop and Pentecostalism; more specifically, their way of doing worship. Over the course of my life, I have had the opportunity to sit in on numerous Pentecostal worship services, including a Pentecostal church service right in my hometown of Providence, Rhode Island.

In my introduction, I mentioned a Neo-Pentecostal church that goes by the name of Praise Tabernacle Church. This church, considered non-denominational by its followers, resembles many Pentecostal churches that I've visited because of how they spend more time worshiping through music (with a live band, choir and an occasional solo artist) than anything else. Following worship service, the pastor would preach for about an hour (sometimes more), then they would conclude with more songs. This would be followed by an intense emotional prayer (again, that concept of "feeling" the Holy Spirit).

Throughout most of the worship service and prayer, a lot of physical body movement took place. This was followed by a lot of demonstrative worship. Some of those same experiences, which included shouting, smiling, yelling, and in some cases, crying, were comparable to the energy that was felt during Critical Resistance's block party event.

There were several MC's that participated in this event. And some of those MC's appeared to be preaching by improvising a prayer through rhyming. For me, it appeared to be no different than a pastor who was preaching about our vices, discontent with the world's super powers, and most importantly, the recognition of God in our lives.

What I also found to be interesting was the wide ranging backgrounds of these MC's—young and old; Black and Latino/a college students; formerly incarcerated men and women; and professors of local colleges. This diversity emphasized the egalitarian element to Pentecostalism, as it displayed Holy Spirit parity when worshiping. In other words, everyone had the opportunity to express their gifts equally, as opposed to *just* the pastor.

As I had mentioned earlier, spiritual gifts are an important element of Pentecostalism, especially when it comes to their demonstration during worship. Consequently, one of the highlights throughout that evening occurred when a local MC by the name of "D-Nice" was being enticed by the audience to freestyle. Now, I have encountered many freestyles in my life, and have participated in my fair share. But certainly, in the world of Hip-hop, the art of the freestyle may serve as the truest rite of passage.

For me, free-styling is an improvisational form of rhyming, performed with few or no previously composed lyrics. It reflects a direct mapping of the mental state and performing situation of the artist. It is non-scripted, non-rehearsed, uncut, and the rawest form of Hip-hop that one can experience. Given this characteristic of free-styling, I see it resembling a lot of what Pentecostals refer to as "speaking in tongues," or *glossolalia*. This is another type of worship (or prayer) that is associated with Pentecostal worship service.

In his book *Catholic Pentecostalism*, René Laurentin discusses how there are multiple ways of understanding the word *glossolalia*. He states that "in some of these varied expressions the word "tongue" alone, without an accompanying verb, means the gifts of tongues, as in I Corinthians 12:10 [*genē glōssōn*, "types of tongues]' 13:8; 14:22."[48] He further goes to add that:

> "*Glōssa* is likewise ambiguous, since it can mean 'language' in a very broad sense, that is, any kind of utterance [presumably intended for communication], as when we speak of the 'language of animals.' Or it can mean 'language' in the narrower sense of phonemes constructed into words and arranged according to a grammar."[49]

Trying to define speaking in tongues is as comprehensive as trying to describe the *experiences* that are felt when speaking in tongues. Speaking in tongues, like spirituality, is therefore difficult to put into words. Nonetheless, in the Pentecostal tradition, "speaking in tongues" is not only viewed as a gift from God, but it is also another way of doing worship.

The ability to MC in the Hip-hop culture is in itself a gift, but what is even more interesting about this gift is that anyone can do it. Like most of the Pentecostal church worship services I have attended, the spirit "pushes" people to speak in tongues as part of worshiping God. Therefore, the freestyle sessions at Critical Resistance's block party had inevitably

---

[48]   René Laurentin, *Catholic Pentecostalism*, (New York: Doubleday & Company, Inc., 1977), 62. ·

[49]   *Id.*, 63.

brought with it a similar ("push") spirit because it compelled an MC by the name of D-Nice, to perform—this spirit was also seen in how the crowd ecstatically reacted toward his performance.

It was the audience response, followed by an emotional response to D-Nice rhyming, that I associate free-styling with "speaking in tongues." After all, René Laurentin agrees to the analogy I make between free-styling and "speaking in tongues" when he states that:

> "Some compare *glossolalia* to the various levels of non-conceptual expressions: poetic and artistic expression, the automatic writing of the surrealist, lettrist poems (an aesthetic invention), and the cries and other utterances used in psychotherapy as helps in attaining inner freedom. In short, the comparison is with all the forms of irrational or inspired language."[50]

When it is all said and done, "speaking in tongues," emotions, gifts, stage and microphone come together to create the worship ambiance of both Pentecostals and Hip-hop culture. Both resemble a form of worship because they both invite people from the community to express themselves in a manner that compels them to speak and to move to the power of the spirit.

The power of the spirit is translated into these spiritual gifts that are made accessible to everyone (not just the pastor). This helps us to explain why Hip-hop, like Pentecostals, has no hierarchical structure because it allows anyone to express themselves freely, which means there is no specific emphasis on how worship is to be conducted.

In his chapter *Two Models of Christian Worship*, Shawn Madigan describes worship as being both "a pattern of cultural and counter-cultural"[51] development. If this is the case, then worship, to an extent, has its relevance in social action in the same way that emotion "encourages us to *act* in conformity with it."[52] In my previous chapter, I mentioned how spirituality not only contains an intellectual element, but also contains

---

[50]   *Id.*, 70.

[51]   Shawn Madigan, *Spirituality Rooted in Liturgy* (Washington D.C: The Pastoral Press, 1988), 92.

[52]   Roberts, 22.

an emotional element. And what this emotional element does is in fact compel us, the Hip-hop culture, to act.

To act, in this case, implies a worship that "pushes" us to come together to recognize God's love for us—through prayer. It's from this act of praying, according to Walter Wink, "where an indispensible means to engage creates a Power."[53] Part of this power that comes with prayer includes a healing element that joins a person when he/she is communicating to God his/her feelings and thoughts. In some cases, praying allows people to express their concerns about a current circumstance(s) that they are undergoing, while in other cases, it may compel the person to give thanks to God for the many blessings that He has given to them.

Indeed, prayer is powerful. Prayer, for some, is *the* best way to communicate with God. Not surprisingly, it has been said that singing is like praying to God three-times because in singing, you put more emphasis into body, heart and soul for your worship—in other words, you are not just using words to pray. With that said, I would also include rhyming into this analogy because it too is like praying three times over, especially when you take into account the emotional and intellectual delivery that these MC's give to his/her audience when they "spit those rhymes" from the heart.

Prayer, and its power, is part of that act, or force; it permits youth to come together and worship in a manner that is more appealing to their culture—Hip-hop. Hip-hop is what draws these youths to create a church within themselves—beyond the four walls of the church and into the broader horizons of the streets. After all, Walter Wink said it best when he stated that:

> "Prayer is never a private inner act disconnected from day-to-day realities. It is, rather, the interior battlefield where the decisive victory is won before any engagement in the outer world is even possible."[54]

And since Hip-hop does this in the name of Jesus Christ and/or the Holy Spirit, it becomes worthy of being named worship, with prayer.

---

[53] Walter Wink, *The Powers that Be* (New York: Augsburg Fortress, 1998), 181.

[54] *Id.*, 181.

A well-known MC from Chicago, Kanye West, captured this concept of prayer as a way of elevating Jesus Christ in a song that he entitled, *Jesus Walks*. In it, Kanye rhymes in a way that almost appears to be prayer-like, as he talks about his personal struggles as a famous artist who is trying to understand his current relationship with Jesus Christ. He goes on to say the following:

"Now hear ye hear ye want to see Thee more clearly/
I know He hear me when my feet get weary/
Cause we're the almost nearly extinct/
We rappers are role models we rap we don't think/
I ain't here to argue about His facial features/
Or here to convert atheists into believers/
I'm just trying to say the way school need teachers/
The way Kathie Lee needed Regis that's the way I need Jesus/
So here go my single dog radio needs this/
They say you can rap about anything except for Jesus/
That means guns, sex, lies, video tapes/
But if I talk about God my record won't get played, Huh?/
Well let this take away from all of my spins/
Which will probably take away from my ends/
Then I hope this take away from my sins/
And bring the day that I'm dreaming about/
Next time I'm in the club everybody screaming out!/
Jesus Walks!"[55]

Not surprisingly, this song by Kanye West did in fact receive a lot of radio play (contrary to what he thought) and became a success in the music scene in the year 2004. Therefore, this song is an example of how prayer is, after all, powerful; even when it's done in a non-traditional and commercialized way.

This also goes to show us that prayer, like worship, can also be done in diverse ways. Liturgy, when examined closely, is actually no different. In his book, *Spirituality Rooted in Liturgy,* Shawn Madigan defines Christian liturgy as being "the loving embrace of all people by Jesus Christ."[56] He

---

[55] Kanye West, *Jesus Walks,* The College Dropout, Roc-A-Fella/Island Def Jam Records, 2004.

[56] Madigan, 177.

further goes to add that, "a plurality of structures, of ministries, of use of gifts, and of rules of order emerged as a function of cultural and religious differences."[57]

Shawn Madigan recognized the influences of culture, society and the various interpretations of Jesus (and His teachings) as emblems for doing liturgy, distinctly. Shawn Madigan's understanding of liturgy is based on how he looks at Paul the Apostle's missionary work. Each church that Paul established, which Shawn Madigan referred to as "Domestic Churches,"[58] created a distinct contribution and dialogue for liturgical life and practice.

For example, "in Corinth, Paul raises some injunctions (I Cor. 11:2-26; I Cor. 14:33-36) on how the Isis cultic practice had had formative effects upon many Christians, former practitioners of the Isis cult."[59] This had an effect on the way this particular community practiced their own liturgy because it brought with it cultic practices that went against formative Christian practices:

> "The cultic practice of honoring the goddess Isis allowed for women in prophetic ecstasy to shout out magical incantations and then let their hair down to effect their magical incantations. In Jewish cultic practice (Lev. 13:45, Nm. 5:18) women let their hair down as a symbol of uncleanness. To avoid symbolic confusion in the Corinthian community, Paul insists that women keep their hair up [or cover their heads], remain silent, and that order be observed in assemblies."[60]

Some might interpret what Paul *meant* to say here differently. Nevertheless, it is important to note how Paul tried to accommodate these "domestic churches," or communities, in a manner that best represented their social needs—which also reflected their liturgical, or public worship, needs. This was practiced in Rome, Macedonia and Thessalonia.

Shawn Madigan also discusses various liturgical distinctions continued today as seen in various locations throughout the world. For example,

---

[57] *Id.*, 183.

[58] *Id.*, 178.

[59] *Id.*, 178.

[60] *Id.*, 177.

Shawn Madigan tells how in the country of Brazil churches—both Protestant and Roman Catholic—have been influenced by Liberation Theology. I shall explain, he says that, "the context of liberation theology has provided the theological basis for communal visions—and actions for—justice in the church and in the surrounding communities."[61]

For example, people who have been martyred (or killed because they fought for the "rights of the poor and/or faith") have become honored by their communities in an almost saint-like capacity. Consequently, prayers of intercession—of these martyrs—have been incorporated into the liturgical rituals of these communities. Likewise, distinctions in liturgical practices can be seen all over the world, including places like Eastern Africa, the Philippines and Europe.[62]

Ultimately, however, Paul the Apostle, under the guidance of Jesus Christ, had a vision. He tried to bring together all of the communities under one banner: Christianity. Yet, people continued to perceive Jesus in light of their own socio-political realities. This has had a major impact on how people worship, pray and do liturgy among the various Christian communities (i.e. worshiping the Isis Cultic practices). Today, as members of the Twenty-First Century community, worship continues to be practiced in a distinct way; Hip-hop music and its culture is a prime example of that.

Whether it's conveying the Gospel through Hip-hop lyrics, or moving your body for Jesus Christ through break dancing; all appear to create a space that is worthy enough to be labeled worship. It is in the power of worship, which Walter Wink alludes to, that allows Hip-hop culture and its delivery of the word to attract hundreds, and even thousands, of youth to various churches like the Hip-hop Church of Harlem. On the other hand, this power is also drawing youth into non-traditional churches of worship, like Holy Hood in the South Bronx, and the smaller short-term venues, like the community gathering, or church, that had taken place at the Critical Resistance event in the Bronx.

Worship, according to Elmer Townes, is done distinctly. And I believe that it should be done differently because we are all different. We see

---

[61]   *Id.*, 184.

[62]   For further discussion on this topic, please see Teresa Berger, *Dissident Daughters: Feminist Liturgies in Global Context* (Louisville, Kentucky: Westminster John Knox Press: 2001).

this distinction of worship within the Hip-hop community because each church worships differently according to their own respective communities; like it was for the communities that Paul the Apostle tried to establish throughout the Mediterranean. At the same time, there does remain a common theme between worship, prayer and liturgy—action.

Hip-hop Forum 2009 at Columbia University. From left to right: Danny AKA Mystery, Omar Fisher, Me, Pastor Din Tolbert, Nicole Ortiz, Daniel Gaztambide, and Rev. Dr. Josef Sorett.

Like spirituality, Christian worship allows the congregation to experience an emotion and an intellect that encourages them to take action. It is in this "call to action" that inspires the community(s) to build and maintain its church through its various ministerial works. In other words, the gifts of the spirit, combined with the ritual offerings of worship, prayer and liturgy, is what in fact describes the major characteristics of what it means to be the church. If this is so, then is it fair to say that Hip-hop culture, in fact, does create a spiritual space for these marginalized youth, as it resembles the various other Christian churches that are in existence today.

But to make such a claim, we first need to try to answer the following questions: What does it mean to be a "church?" What is its function? And how has it been defined over the years? If in fact worship, prayer, liturgy and spirituality does push us to act, than how has Hip-hop acted in the name of God? In other words, has Hip-hop been used as a ministry . . . for change? Let us conclude our journey by trying to answer these questions. Let us proceed.

CHAPTER 4:

Hip-hop and the Church

Allah's the most gracious/
He made the universe the most spacious/
Seen and heard in all places/ but still appears faceless/
Embraces all races/ all caste and all cases/
In every spec of life he's the substance of all traces/

The answer to all questions/ the spark of all suggestions/
Of righteousness, the pathway to the road of perfection/
Who gives you all and never ask more of you/
The faithful companion that fights every war with you/
Before the mortal view of the pre-historical, historical/
He's the all and all, you searching for the oracle/
Of mission impossible/ purely philosophical/
But you call Him on your death bed when you laying in the hospital/

And as you play all day like the grasshopper who work and toil/
Like armies of ants carrying stones of soil/
Building a home for themselves and storing food/
At night we praise Allah and adore the moon/
In sync like the flow of the Nile/ the growth of a child/
Only fearing GOD, we create a ghost with a smile/
That which is spirit is spirit, which is flesh is flesh/
Meaning life has no partnership with death/

Yo, I've been highly misunderstood by those who met us/
They had ears of corn and heads of lettuce/
Mentally dead/ essentially lead/ by the false teachings/
And eventually pledge their allegiance/
To that which was against them and exempt them from the truth/
Then juiced them and pimp them . . . .

So that the church can rise/ while their babies home hungry covered with
flies/
Trying to harness the wind/
Allah's the father from without and within/
On Christ return, who will announce him?/
Every tree is numbered, but who can count them?/
The name of all things on this world, who can pronounce them?/

Allah is the father of all, why do you doubt him?/

—Rza
From the song entitled *Sunlight*

The Church does not authentically attain consciousness of itself except in the perception of this total presence of Christ in His Spirit in humanity.

—Gustavo Gutiérrez
A Theology of Liberation

There have always been people (true, small groups—individuals) who knew that the basic words of the church are not "to call back" or "to call toward one," but rather, "to go out," "to seek," "to find." These words they have translated into their own lives. They did go out, across the threshold, although not in this case to "the ends of the earth" across the ocean, but rather across the street, from the one nation into the other.

—J.C. Hoekendijk
Church Inside Out

A proper ordering of the whole of community life according to God's standards is an essential part of the Church's mission. Christians are to penetrate the earthly kingdoms, transform them, and bring them more into accord with the will of God. Christ is taken to the world, not only to transform personal lives but to transform the social structures within which Christians live and move.

—David Fraser and Tony Campolo
Sociology Through the Eyes of Faith

W e have come to the final destination of our journey—putting it all together. I've discovered how Hip-hop's socio-historical reality has influenced a spirit that creates a space for these marginalized youth to come together and worship God in solidarity. I've described these "spiritual spaces" (created in a non-conventional way) as an example of Holy Hood in the South Bronx. In other examples, we have seen the Hip-hop culture convened under a more traditional and institutionalized arena—where Hip-hop still is the center of all worship and doctrine. The Hip-hop Church of Harlem serves as a prime example of this approach.

Most interesting is how churches are being created (and recreated) whenever Hip-hop culture presents itself to the masses in an overtly public capacity. An example of this was the aforementioned Critical Resistance event in the South Bronx that was discussed in the previous chapter. To the naked eye, this event was nothing more than a form of entertainment. But looking beyond the exterior, and actually examine this event in its entirety, one can see how this environment is in fact a recipe for a spiritual experience. It bears resemblance to past churches and their original missions here on earth.

Before I explain what I mean by "resembling the original churches," we first need to ask ourselves the following questions: What *were* the original intentions of the church? What was (and still are) its function(s)? And finally, who or what has defined the church, for us both historically and for today? Attempting to answer these questions well help us to answer the most important question to this topic: What exactly *is* the church?

Me lecturing at my Hip-hop forum at Union Theological Seminary at Columbia University in New York City.

The church (specifically, the Christian Church and all of its denominations) has historically undergone what can be described as a "funnel phase." After Jesus' death, there existed countless sects who would gather together and discuss the teachings of Jesus Christ based on their own interpretations. These first Christians practiced their faith throughout the Mediterranean area and beyond.

However, when the religious councils began to take shape and commence some 300 year later, things changed. The first council was convened by Constantine the Great, Christians became "united," or sucked into the narrowing of the funnel, as one universal apostolic church.[63] However, the pressure of the funnel became so tight that it began to expand outward again, resulting in the Reformation Period 1,200 years later.[64] And so, the church, beginning with Reformers such as Martin Luther and John

---

[63]   For further discussion on this, please see R. Gerberding and J. H. Moran Cruz, *Medieval Worlds* (New York: Houghton Mifflin Company, 2004).

[64]   For further discussion on this, please see Carter Lindberg, *The Reformation Theologians: Introduction to Theology in the Early Modern Period* (Oxford: Blackwell Publishers, Inc., 2002).

Calvin, began to take "a second look" at itself in light of those conditions that were occurring both within and *outside* of its four walls.

Because the church can be viewed as a "historical movement, and the various churches are themselves historical institutions or societies with a variety of organizational forms," [65] we must then look at the church not only in its broader historical development, like the "funnel phase" example that previously outlined, but also through its sociological development—similar to how Hip-hop's history is described in the first chapter of this thesis.

In other words, we need to examine the church using an ecclesiological lens to better comprehend the true meaning of the/a Church. In his multi-volume book, *Christian Community in History,* Father Roger Haight (a Scholar in Residence at Union Theological Seminary in New York City) defines ecclesiology as "the study of the church in an effort to understand its nature and mission"[66] because "different historical conditions and contexts determine different viewpoints, premises, basic values and methods of approach to the church." [67]

It is from this particular view of the church that Professor Roger Haight separates ecclesiology into two distinct parts: an ecclesiology from below and an ecclesiology from above. With an ecclesiology from above, "one can make a direct appeal to the New Testament in understanding the Church." [68] In other words, by looking into the life and times of Jesus Christ and His "stance" on the "church," we see how authority (in this case, mainline churches) has developed and assembled its own doctrinal belief based upon interpretation of Jesus in light of the four Gospels.

---

[65] Roger Haight, *Christian Community in History: Volume 1, Historical Ecclesiology* (New York: The Continuum International Publishing Group, Inc., 2004), 21.

[66] *Id.,* 17.

[67] *Id.,* 17.

[68] *Id.,* 21.

The Bronx.

An ecclesiology from below, however, is defined as "the Church existing not apart from the world, but as part of the world, and in such a way that the world is not outside it, but inside it." [69] This particular view makes the church sound like it is always in constant flux because in reality, the world is, historically and socially, *always* shifting. It is from this definition of an "ecclesiology from below" that we focus the remainder for this chapter; because it is in this particular characterization of the church that one can see Hip-hop embodying.

According to Wes Howard-Brook's book, *The Church before Christianity,* for the "Israelite elite living in the diaspora among Greeks, the image of *ekklēsia,* had been at least in part, transformed from the assembly of 'all Israel' to an *urban* body composed of the intellectual [and economic] movers and shakers."[70] *Ekklēsia,* is the Greek word for a "community gathering or assembly." Author Wes Howard-Brook makes

---

[69] *Id.,*59.

[70] Wes Howard-Brook, *The Church Before Christianity* (Maryknoll, New York: Orbis Books, 2001), 28.

note of this earlier version of the church, or *ekklēsia,* when he references the Book of Sirach.[71]

But what makes this perspective on the *ekklēsia,* as an "assembly of all Israel," so special is that it encompasses all of the community, not just Israelites themselves, but secular figures as well; including politicians, statesmen, engineers, but not all. So in essence, the early community gatherings of Israel were themselves diverse in societal roles, not so much diverse as we'd like it (because it lacked diversity in ethnicity, sexuality, race and class) but diverse at least for the time being.

This is the kind of church that Roger Haight alluded to when he spoke about an "ecclesiology from below" because it lacked doctrinal dictatorship, which evolves later. In other words, the church is a movement from the people on the ground, or from below. According to Wes-Howard Brook, the early Israelites proved "works from the ground" when they allowed secular communities into the decision-making practices of the church, and more specifically, the synagogue.

MC Spirit Child performing at the Critical Resistance rally.

---

[71] The Book of Sirach is a work from the second century BCE, originally written in Hebrew. The book is included in the Septuagint and is accepted as part of the Biblical canon by Catholics, Eastern Orthodox, and most Oriental Orthodox, but not by most Protestants.

The ancient Israelites integration of the sacred with the secular, or church with society, became the same juncture at which the first followers of Jesus Christ encountered in antiquity. One of the first Christians to experience this firsthand was Paul the Apostle. In the previous chapter, I mentioned briefly how Paul helped to resolve the cultic practices of the early Christian community in Corinth. This was one of the challenges the first Christians had to contend with—how to accommodate the existing diverse social constructs while adhering to the teachings of Jesus Christ.

Shawn Madigan, the same author who gave us an account of Paul's missionary work in Corinth, described each of these encounters as "converts associating themselves with a household church."[72] In his book, *Spirituality Rooted in Liturgy*, Shawn Madigan defines each of these "household churches" that Paul established as "domestic churches."[73] Each of these "domestic churches" could be identified as being distinct, self-sustaining and community oriented. Shawn Madigan further adds that:

"As the Christian community grew in size, the household character of ecclesia [or church] was retained through formation of other churches. The practice reflects the emphasis the early church put on strong *communal bonding*. These bonds were considered crucial in encouraging and safeguarding the quality of life expected by Christians."[74]

Consequently, it became clear to Paul that his main priority should be in trying to *build and sustain these communities* of early Christians. Part of this recognition comes from acknowledging the diversity that was found within each "domestic house." Shawn Madigan goes on to say that "this plurality of the ecclesia was still considered to be one church. And so, Paul addressed one letter to the variety of the churches, namely, Rome and Corinth."[75] In other words, although Paul did in fact acknowledge the diversity that was found within the various churches, he also recognized that:

---

[72] Madigan, 179.

[73] *Id.*, 178.

[74] *Id.*, 179.

[75] *Id.*,179.

"The churches did not belong to the people who were its members, or to the district in which they were located. Paul's churches belonged to the One who has called the community into being [I Cor. 1:1; 2 Cor. 1:1; 1 Cor. 10:32, 11:22; Rom. 16:16)."[76]

Coincidently, it was Paul who was assigned to spread the Good News to the other nations—the uncircumcised and gentiles—while the Apostle Peter preached to the circumcised (Acts 15:2 and Galatians 2:1). Paul's commitment to unity and spreading of the Gospel is the reason why I reference him as prime example of what Hip-hop culture is doing today. Paul felt compelled to spread the word to all nations. Similarly, we see advocates of the Hip-hop culture today using the word (MC-ing) to spread the message of God to *all* nations.

In their book, *Sociology through the Eyes of Faith,* David Fraser and Tony Campolo describe Paul as:

"Focusing sharply on the "indifference" of religion to culture and social status where the people of God are concerned. No cultural or social distinctive prevent any person from being fully a part of the Body of Christ. 'There is neither Jew nor Greek, slave nor free, male or female, for you are all one in Christ Jesus. If you belong to Christ, then you are Abraham's seed and heirs according to the promise (Galatians 3:28-29; see also I Corinthians 9; Romans 14).'[77]

How David Fraser and David Campolo described Paul is the way in which I describe the Hip-hop culture and its participants—different. But unlike the Hip-hop culture (which supports and encourages diversity by not compacting it into one group, place or person), Paul's emphasis on diversity becomes overridden by doctrine, rules and regulations, and orthodoxy as a way of unifying the various (and distinct) churches that were spread all throughout and around the Mediterranean Sea.

---

[76]   *Id..*, 179.

[77]   David A. Fraser and Tony Campolo, *Sociology: Through the Eyes of Faith* (New York: HarperCollins Publishers, Ltd., 1992), 198.

As mentioned previously, it was in the beginning of the Fourth Century when the Roman Catholic Church first attempted to sustain this "unity"—between these diverse "houses"—that Paul established. However, the Reformation Period of the Sixteenth Century once again proved the importance in diversity when it broke away from the Roman Catholic Church. Subsequently, what would follow for the next five hundred years included building these distinct "domestic houses" into their own "cultural, social, and prior religious imagination."[78] One of those "domestic houses" can be seen today in the Hip-hop culture. Like those communities in the First Century, Hip-hop has also reinterpreted God or Jesus Christ based on its own socio-historical reality.

In other words, it was in the public street corners and avenues of the South Bronx where we see Hip-hops' "domestic houses" first beginning to flourish in the Twentieth Century. And like the first Christian "churches," Hip-hop's priority was, and always has been, in community building and assembling (*ekklēsia*). One of those churches can be seen today in the South Bronx—Holy Hood. Similar to the churches of antiquity, Holy Hood's long lasting tradition has been to gather all those nations (i.e. diverse races, sexes, cultures), particularly those left in the margins of society—marginalized youth—together. This includes using Hip-hop culture as an intermediary in building and sustaining viable communities in the name of Jesus Christ.

For example, one of the ways Paul the Apostle tried to unite his communities into solidarity was by replicating Jesus' Last Supper with his Disciples. In other words, a meal became a vital component to these First Century "domestic houses," as it helped to recreate the fellowship that helped to bond Jesus Christ with His disciples.

As I mentioned above, every Friday night before service began, Holy Hood staff convened its congregants to join them for an agape meal. I had the opportunity to sit in on one of these agape meals. I will never forget how many tables were used to accommodate so many of God's children that night: Black, White, Latino/a, gay, lesbian, gang members, former prison inmates, college students, dope dealers and others shared the table. It reminded me of what Paul did "to remind the Corinthian community that the Lord's meal *belongs to all.*"[79] On that day, like every other Friday,

---

[78]   Madigan, 180.

[79]   *Id.,* 180.

everyone brought food to share with the rest of the congregation. And if, for whatever reason, a person was unable to bring in any food, they were still welcomed to what Reverend Raymond Rivera calls, "God's House."

Another "domestic house" that flourished in the South Bronx is called Grace Place. With meetings every other Wednesday evening, Grace Place is just one of the many services that Youth Ministries for Peace and Justice (YMPJ) brings to the Morrison/Soundview community. The purpose of Grace Place is to encourage youth to come together and dialogue. They talk amongst themselves about the growing pains of being a young adult and how their own faith in God helps to navigate through these experiences. In most cases, Hip-hop music is used as a way to express those feelings, including but not limited to: spoken word, graffiti art work and dance.

The Bronx River Projects (one of the historical cornerstones of
Hip-hop culture and music).

As a former youth mentor and facilitator of Grace Place at YMPJ, I always encouraged my youth to lead discussions in this space (after all, this space is intended for them). I considered this space to be spiritual and therefore, church. I wholeheartedly believe this to be true. I will never forget a young woman who would always come to Grace Place to rhyme about how she wanted to commit suicide. I would notice this common thread in her lyrics, as she would often refer to her frustrations in life and how it forced her to think about how it takes her life away.

One day she came up to me and told me that she in fact did contemplate committing suicide, but instead, she utilized this space to release her anger—which would have otherwise been used to take her life away. I honestly believe that my influence as a mentor encouraged her to write and rhyme about committing suicide rather than have her actually commit the act. Church and God's spirit intervenes in the lives of these youth—the most prominent form of Divine Intervention.

Interfaith crosses displayed in front of the Youth Ministries for Peace and Justice house in the South Bronx.

Traveling beyond the South Bronx now, we find another "domestic house," only this one, ironically, is called "Tha House."[80] This community

---

[80] The House is an aggressive, Christ-centered, urban, youth-driven, culturally-relevant, biblically accurate, community-empowering, family-friendly hip-hop ministry that cultivates and empowers youth living on the Westside of Chicago with a sustainable faith. We present the gospel of Christ in a real, practical, holistic and relational way in order to transform the lives of youth living in today's hip-hop culture.

from the West Side of Chicago meets three Saturdays a month for worship, prayer, rhymes, dance and finally, a meal. Tha House's motto is based on the Christian Bible's Book of Psalms chapter 127 verse 1. This Old Testament scripture reads as follows: "Unless the Lord builds the house, those who build it labor in vain. Unless the Lord watches over the city, the watchman stays awake in vain."[81]

The West Side of Chicago has historically undergone the same social hostilities that the South Bronx has encountered during the growth of Hip-hop: police misconduct, gangs, drugs, poverty, high prison rates and high school dropout rates, oftentimes resulting in a lower quality of life for inhabitants of the region. Thankfully, a "domestic house," or Tha House, was erected as a way to draw these marginalized youth into an alternative community—one that centers itself around God's word, through Hip-hop of course.

Tha House not only attracts about five hundred youth every week, but it is also the first of its kind in Chicago. Under the supervision of Pastor Phil Jackson, youth from Chicago and all over the United States, have either joined or visited this spiritual place of Hip-hop culture: rhyming, DJ-ing, B-boying and B-girling, graffiti and spoken word. For the average person looking from the outside, Tha House is nothing more than a Hip-hop concert in "the hood." But when one takes the time to see how youth are embracing Hip-hop culture as a tool for performing important youth ministry work, you will see Tha House as being more than just its four walls and music—but simply, church.

This is why ministry, along with community building and a meal, *is* what defines the church. As part of the evangelization process, Paul the Apostle assigned various tasks to its communities, or ministries. Like Holy Hood and YMPJ in the South Bronx, Tha House in Chicago also responded to the youth by utilizing Hip-hop as *the* ministry for spreading God's message to all nations. When describing ministerial work in the church, Professor Roger Haight says the following:

"Ministries respond to needs; they actualize the community assuming responsibility for interacting with its environment, the needs of its members, and the goals for which it was

---

[81]   The New Oxford Annotated Bible, Revised Standard Version, (New York: Oxford University Press), 1973.

founded . . . . the moral identity of the early church was a synthesis of many social and cultural influences that evolved over the first two centuries." [82]

Ministry is such an important component of the church. Yet, most Christian churches today, no matter what their denominational affiliation is, continue to lack a well–constructed youth ministry program (this is assuming they have a youth ministry program at all). In having served as a youth minister for some time, I have seen this happen repeatedly. In response to this problem I have made several attempts with various churches about considering utilizing Hip-hop as part of their ministry in reaching out to both current and prospective youth. Regrettably, I was turned down by many clergy and lay people alike because they viewed Hip-hop as being part of the problem (i.e. vices and violence), and not the solution.

Youth organizing and strategizing in the Bronx.

Another reason why Hip-hop is not popular among clergy is because of the "risk" that comes with bringing to the church those with

---

[82]   Haight, 100.

checkered pasts: former gang members, high school drop outs, and drug abusers—assuming Paul the Apostle and Jesus Christ never dealt with "those types" of people during their public ministry. And so, gaining the respect and support of the church, especially the institutional church, continues to be a hard fought battle for me and my Hip-hop culture.

But then again, when I think about Hip-hop's challenge to be accepted as a ministry, I start to think about how Jesus Christ Himself was confronted and challenged by the powers and principalities of the institutional church. In fact, most of Jesus' attempt to dialogue with the church, or more specifically the Temple, ended unsuccessfully.

For example, in the Gospel of Saint Luke, Jesus was physically removed by a crowd from the synagogue (Luke 4:28-30). In the Gospel of Saint John; however, he was physically attacked by people in the synagogue (John 2:13-25); and finally, in the Gospel of Saint Mark, He predicted the destruction of the Temple (Mark 13:1-4). Now, there are many ways to interpret these Biblical excerpts. But the point is Jesus' interaction with the institutional powers is what eventually forced Him to do most of His ministerial work outside—in the streets.

As I mentioned above, in Luke 2:28-30, Jesus was literally rejected by the congregation in the synagogue and thrown into the streets where he was almost killed. Shortly before that occurred, Jesus had read an excerpt from the Book of Isaiah in the Old Testament. In it, Isaiah had prophesized the coming of the Lord and how He would minister to the poor and the oppressed in order to bring freedom to them all (Isaiah 61:1-2). As soon as Jesus finished reading that Biblical passage, He received an extermination threat by those who were present on that day. Surely enough, immediately following this threat, Jesus Christ began his ministry—a public ministry that would change the course of history forever.

And so, the question we should be asking ourselves is: Do we want to give Hip-hop the same fate that Jesus Christ eventually endured (his crucifixion) because of our own ignorance to see the potential that it has to also minister to the poor, oppressed and marginalized youth of our time? According to the youth at Praise Tabernacle Church in Cranston, Rhode Island, the answer to this question is a resounding 'No!'

Praise Tabernacle, as I mentioned in previous chapters, is a non-denominational and Neo-Pentecostal Church that serves the community of greater Providence, Rhode Island. Pastor Noel is their youth minister and he, along with other youth members, coordinates an outreach program called "Search and Rescue." This ministry, which is part of their "Thursday Night Teens" (TNT) Program, has gained a reputation throughout the city because it is one of the few churches in that area that works with the homeless (Pastor Levi takes care of this department); additionally, it is the only church that reaches out to the youth in one of the most precarious neighborhoods in Providence. On any given Saturday, you can catch these youth ministers utilizing the Hip-hop culture to convey the message of God in places like the Manton Projects and the Chad Brown Housing Projects.

Danny AKA Mystery getting ready to spit it in the booth.

These two projects are in one of the most crime-ridden areas in Providence. Yet, youth from Praise Tabernacle Church continue to come to these places to rhyme, do spoken word, break dance, provide food, enjoy prize give-a-ways and preach the Gospel to these marginalized communities in Rhode Island. While it may appear to the average person that these community gatherings are just fun and games, it is actually public ministry in motion because it provides all the right ingredients for taking the church into the streets.

Similar to what Paul the Apostle did in the First Century, these youth from Praise Tabernacle took the words, and spirit, of Jesus Christ and brought it to the public places of the city (the housing project court yards to be exact) and created their own community gathering, or church. The enthusiasm from these young men and women from Praise Tabernacle Church is what eventually drew people to these charismatic forms of preaching (or rhyming), and human videos (which are scripted plays with music in the background), which were then followed by a meal. And *everyone,* no matter who they were, had a chance to eat at this dinner table—or God's House!

While this "domestic house" was under construction in Rhode Island, another one was being built down in Miami, Florida. The First Presbyterian Church of Miami has a youth ministry program, which meets bi-weekly, called "Catalyst Miami." Hip-hop fan and Christian missionary Joel Stigale developed this ministry after growing up in a crime infested neighborhood in Miami-Dade County. Raised by missionaries, Stigale's goal, like Praise Tabernacle Church, was to help bring the Gospels of Jesus to the streets while providing outreach services to troubled youth.

In other words, this ministry is not solely based on trying to evangelize these marginalized youth, as much as it is trying to focus on the artistry element of the Hip-hop culture—graffiti. The challenges that come with introducing graffiti art work as an alternative to street life is what Joel Stigale describes as:

> "A lot of these guys are dealing with society as they've had to deal with it. They don't have any hope. They don't have anybody they can really trust. So, they're looking for an escape, and for many of them that escape is usually some sort of drug or alcohol abuse, and they end up through break dance or through painting getting into a better frame of life as far as taking care of themselves."[83]

Joel Stigale is absolutely right. In reality, it is hard working with youth that don't believe in a tomorrow, let alone Jesus Christ (believe me I have encountered this hurdle numerous times throughout my own ministry). But that *is* the challenge that comes with reaching out to those places where the institutional churches are refusing to go to.

This is why I believe God brought Hip-hop into this world, so it too can contribute to the ministerial efforts of bringing heaven here on "earth as it is in heaven." Like Paul the Apostle, Hip-hop builds communities, or, what Shawn Madigan refers to as, "domestic houses." On the one hand, you have the institutionalized churches of Hip-hop, like the Hip-hop Church of Harlem. As I mentioned in previous chapters, this church has its own style of worship, prayer and liturgy, which is nevertheless interpreted via the Hip-hop culture. But at the same time, this church has its structures: dogma, doctrine, and rituals. Similar to the orthodox traditions of the African Methodist Episcopal Zion Church, which by the way, has its origins in New York City.[84]

---

[83] Lucia Orozco, "Hip-Hop Urban Lifestyle Meets a Higher Power." *Miami Herald,* NorthWest Miami Edition, January 2009. www.miamiherald.com/news/miami_dade/northwest/story/844464.html (Accessed 2 February 2009).

[84] For further discussion of this, please see: James Grant Wilson, ed., *The Memorial History of the City of New York from Its First Settlement to the Year 1892* (New York: New-York History Company), 1893.

On the other side of the spectrum, Holy Hood, Grace Place and Tha House, are churches that are more non-traditional and independent. Therefore, they resemble more closely the *ekklesias*, or community gatherings, of the First Century—before they became institutionalized. These churches, like Paul's churches, focused more on community building, fellowship, and a meal, which is based on the idea of building God's 'Kin-dom,' (which is not to be confused with Kingdom, as that implies a hierarchical system) here on earth.

This view of the church comes to us again from Professor Roger Haights theory on an "ecclesiology from above" and an "ecclesiology from below." Again, it is from the latter of the two definition of the church where we see these non-traditional churches crystallize the meaning of social/earthly participation of God's true church. In other words, these particular churches of Hip-hop, according to Professor Roger Haight, have understood the:

"Adjustment, change, development, expansion, pluralism and authority that are all reflected in the early church, which characterizes the very structure of a living institutional community in history."[85]

Of course, this is not to say that the "ecclesiology of the above" viewpoint is any less important, or for that matter, less of a church because it's overly institutionalized.

Because in reality, when you combine the "ecclesiology from above," which is vertical, with an "ecclesiology from below," which is horizontal, it creates an intersection (the cross) between the private ministry (institutional church) and the public ministry (the society, specifically, the marginalized society). This intersection is seen in the various youth ministries that I've mentioned earlier, such as the Catalyst Miami Movement and the Search and Rescue initiative in Rhode Island.

---

[85] Haight, 61.

Graffiti art work in Amsterdam.

Realistically speaking, both of these ministries are getting support from "above;" that is to say, Catalyst Miami is sponsored by the Presbyterian tradition in the same way that Search and Rescue is sponsored by the Pentecostal Charismatic Movements.[86] The latter of the two reaffirms, again, why I've stated that Hip-hop resembles the Pentecostal church more than any other Christian denomination—particularly regarding the acts of worship.

As I mentioned in my introduction, this comparison on Hip-hop and Pentecostalism is based on my observations and participation in the Hip-hop culture. My concluding observations are based on the following cross-analysis: The MC (who acts as the preacher), the stage (the sanctuary), the rhyming (the message, or Gospel), the congregation (the spectators, or audience), and finally, the many "spiritual gifts" that comes with implementing the Hip-hop culture into the churches worship service (i.e. Critical Resistance event; see Chapter 2).

---

[86] For further discussion on this, please see: Stanley M. Burgess and Eduard M. Van Der Maas, eds., *The New International Dictionary of Pentecostal and Charismatic Movements* (Grand Rapids, Michigan: Strang Communications Company), 2002.

Whether or not you believe that the Hip-hop culture is worthy of being called Church is irrelevant. Because a/the church consists of more than orthodoxy, hierarchical systems and physical structures; the church consists of, above all else, fulfilling its ministerial duties through public servitude, companionship and social services. Not just to its current congregants, but toward its prospective ones; especially those who have been left in the margins of society—youth in particular. After all, Professor Roger Haight said it best when he said the following:

> "The church can never be without the ministries it needs to pursue its mission. Ministry is not something that is added onto the community in history. The church *is* its ministry; the church is ministry in act."[87]

It was this same ambition, or spirit, that allowed Paul the Apostle to act and subsequently, establish multiple churches in and around the Mediterranean Sea. Likewise, we saw this same spirit influence the Reformation Period, and now, the culture of Hip-hop.

Therefore, the church and its key players (pastor, clergy, seminaries, and formal) need to begin considering utilizing Hip-hop as a medium to reach out to our marginalized youth who are in fact yearning for righteousness, justice, love, spirituality and God.

This is why Hip-hop culture's effort to gather and to build communities, which first began in the streets of the South Bronx, continues to inspire generations of street disciples that are committed to going out and minister to everyone the love, hope, and struggle of Jesus Christ. And that, for me, is what I consider, more than anything, to be spiritual, worship, ministry, the church and Hip-hop!

---

[87] Haight, 65.

CONCLUSION

*Your people will rebuild the ancient ruins and restore the foundations
of past generations. You will be called the Rebuilder of Broken Walls
and the Restorer of Streets where people live.*

—Isaiah 58:12

I want to conclude this socio-historical, ecclesiological, and spiritual journey of Hip-hop by taking a few moments to reflect on the relationship between Hip-hop and God; specifically through examining the life and times of Jesus Christ. This will help us to understand why Hip-hop is worthy of its place in God's history. Although I am not a theologian, I want to nevertheless give a brief exegesis of the Bible and how it relates to Hip-hop today.

In the Gospel of Saint Matthew in the New Testament, you will find a powerful message from Jesus Christ that states: "Where two or three are gathered together in my name, there am I in the midst of them"[88] (Matthew18:20). What I find interesting about this passage is that Jesus never specifies which name He is referring to? Of course, the most obvious name that He is referring to is Jesus Christ because that was the name given to Him since birth. However, all throughout the Gospels, Jesus (and others) refers to Himself by many names.

Some of those names include the following: Teacher (John 3:2), Advocate (1 John 2:1), Head of the Church (Ephesians 5:23), and Servant (Matthew 12:18). This diversity in designation is what defined Jesus for many people who encountered Him during His time here on earth, not to mention that these titles are what characterize a well-rounded Christian—servant, teacher, advocate, and the like. But I would like to

---

[88]   The New Oxford Annotated Bible, Revised Standard Version, (New York: Oxford University Press), 1973.

add one more name to the above list; a name that I find to be extremely profound. That name is "The Word" (John 1:1).

The Bible is still the best-selling book of all time, all over the world, and the mission of the Gospels is to faithfully convey Jesus' words to humanity. Because Jesus understood the power of his own word, He chose to spend his time ministering in public places, because it was there that *all* of His children came together and interacted with one another at the same time. In regards to this context, the way Jesus originally imagined "the church" may be different than the way we identify it today.

Jesus' commitment to public ministry helps us rethink what He really meant when He said: "Where two or more are gathered, I am there." On the one hand, this statement can be viewed as a blueprint for the church of the future, because wherever Jesus' word is spoken, that is where the church is; it is also where theology, history, salvation and hope intersect. But, on the other hand, the concept of "church" for Jesus was constantly being re-imagined and redefined whenever he encountered people in their own social-political, historical and circumstantial realities.

Praising and Worshiping at the Thursday Night Teens (TNT) service at Praise Tabernacle Church in Cranston, Rhode Island.

In every instance, Jesus' "Word" drew people together and as a result, created a space that was altogether diverse, spiritual and thought provoking. I believe the same powerful "Word" that was used by Jesus Christ to gather communities together in first century Palestine is what currently helps Hip-hop to establish its various churches today. In other words, the Hip-hop culture has created a spiritual public discourse that not only consists of politics, race, history, religion, oppression, classism, and all other "-isms"; it also created a discourse that allows for a more nuanced way of looking at life, ourselves, our community and our relationship with God.

In his book, *Mapping Public Theology: Beyond Culture, Identity and Difference,* Benjamin Valentin discusses implementing a public (and diverse) discourse similar to the one that Jesus' "Word" provoked when he confronted His own diversities: Roman soldiers, the poor, the elite, women, men, pious people, marginalized and disadvantaged people. Valentin refers to this public discourse as none other than a Public Theology. He defines Public Theology as such:

"A public theology should engage in forms of open inquiry and persuasions that do not lapse into authoritarian, parochial modes of argumentation or find their substantiation in 'local reservations of spirit' or cryptic revelatory messages. It must demonstrate the courage to employ critical intelligence, to face up to the inescapable fallibility of human thought and talk without succumbing to sophomoric relativism or wholesale skepticism, and to pursue the difficult trek of open and reasonable dialogue in society. In this sense, theology enters public life not to assert itself, but rather, to participate in the remedying of social injustice and, thus, to create a better society."[89]

"To create a better society"—isn't that the goal of the church? This is why I have a preference for those churches that spend just as much time outside of the church building as they do inside it. It is one thing to bring

---

[89]   Benjamin Valentin, *Mapping a Public Theology: Beyond Culture, Identity and Difference* (New York: Trinity Press International, 2002), 110.

people into the church, but it is another thing when you can bring the church to the people.

Me and MC KRS-One.

I will never forget what was once said by the honorable Reverend Howard Moody, former Senior Pastor at Judson Memorial Church in New York City,[90] and also one of the most socially active clergymen of the twentieth century. Howard stated, "The Church exists primarily for those not in it." It is not surprising to me that most of Jesus' teachings, parables, lessons and miracles happened with acquaintances He made in the streets. And for every human He encountered, He did something to them that was, well, beyond their understanding. This enigmatic quality seems to be the reason that Jesus was able to gather people by His side: to those people he encountered, Jesus' "Word" was not only mentally and physically stimulating, but it was also spiritually inspiring.

This spiritual encounter between Jesus and humanity became the same (holy) spirit that Jesus left behind for His Disciples, and for the world, to

---

90 Judson Memorial Church is deeply rooted in the Free Church, Baptist and UCC traditions. Its senior pastor, Reverend Donna Schaper, and congregants are committed to immigration issues, fair trade and the economy.

embrace and to minister the Good News (1 Thessalonians 4:7-8; John 14:15-18; 1 Peter 1:12). This spiritual encounter also extends to Hip-hop culture, especially in a performance capacity, because of the connection between the audience and the "minister," or performer.

The emotion that arises from these diverse public discourses does in fact create a space that is not only intellectually vigorous and critically analytical, but is also very conscious of the same fundamental values that bind us all together as Christians: love, peace, prayer, reconciliation, hope, humility, humbleness, social justice and recognition of the "Other," bringing us to solidarity, or a oneness. Of course, any person or space that allows for similar words and feelings to be expressed freely in the public sphere (i.e. Hip-hop) is also interposing a high level of emotion and sentiment.

In the fall of 2008, I registered for a class at Union Theological Seminary that was entitled, *Social Ethics as Social Criticism.* This class was facilitated by Professor Gary Dorrien, the Reinhold Niebuhr Professor at Union Theological Seminary. The course required us to study current literature in Christian social ethics by focusing on issues such as race, gender and class. Of course, those same issues became more and more nuanced once we began talking about white supremacy, racial justice, feminist theory, economic justice, the problems of exclusion and the common good.

One can imagine the sort of discussions that emerged from this class and were submerged due to the sensitivity that was found in ethical, political, theological, racial and social issues. This public discourse became even more cumbersome when you take into consideration the diversity that this particular class had—White, Blacks, Latino/a, South East Asians, working class professionals, elders, activists, clergy, young people, gays, lesbians—all sorts of people.

I specifically remember one week when we were assigned a book entitled, *Disrupting White Supremacy From Within,* by Jennifer Harvey, Karen A. Case and Robin Hawley Gorsline. I could tell from the title alone that this book was going to be trouble. Two of our white female colleagues gave a presentation on this book, both making very deep and critical analyses of the content, based on their own personal experiences and social realities as white women growing up in the United States.

Me signing autographs in Medellin, Colombia in South America.

One presenter spoke up about her upbringing in the rural south, and became very emotional as she recalled being disowned by her family, friends and neighbors for branching out culturally and racially. Her associations with Hip-hop music and relationship with a mixed-race person were not issues that her conservative family and friends were prepared to accept. I was very moved by her story; indeed, it was so powerful, that after she finished speaking, there was a silence that filled the room. During this silence, I paused to look around the classroom which, for me, represented the many different faces of our society; those faces were filled with awe, tears, puzzlement and shock.

The following week, I presented my response to another class text, none other than Benjamin Valentin's book, *Mapping Public Theology: Beyond Culture, Identity and Difference.* My presentation began by recognizing the lack of spiritual connectedness that exists in our institutions, in this case, academia (and more specifically, the seminary setting) because spirituality is viewed as being either too irrational or too emotional.

I stated further that our life experiences and stories are vital components in understanding our own lives, our society and our relationship with God. I also shared my own experiences growing up in the "hood," or "ghetto," and how it shaped my outlook in life, essentially acknowledging the power of telling stories, expressing emotion, sharing the wisdom of life experience, and reflecting on my personal relationship with God.

I ended my presentation by publicly thanking my white female colleagues for sharing their stories with the class because for me, it was one of the few times that I felt God present in that room. Consequently, this place, this secular environment, demonstrated to us what Benjamin Valentin described as a Public Theology. Similarly, I see the Hip-hop culture resembling these same feelings and emotions that I, along with my classmates, experienced when we came together to discuss the various social injustices that affect each and every one of us in our daily lives. This Public Theology is where the Hip-hop culture and spirituality convenes.

Unfortunately, this spiritual unity, which I see Hip-hop aiming for, becomes ever so difficult to achieve in the midst of us always fighting for our theological, racial, economical, sexual, gender and sometimes political voices to be heard. As a result, we became forgetful as to how similar we really are as human beings navigating life's harsh realities.

These kind of public discourses, which encourage critical thinking, self-expression or what the Hip-hop culture refers to as "keeping it *real,*" are sometimes looked at negatively by academics, politicians, clergy and others in a position of authority. For some of them, a spirituality that appears to be too emotional and subjective soon becomes theorized, dichotomized and polarized. But when we do take that step to go beyond the superficial rhetoric, academic *and* religious romanticism, and notions of political correctness, we enter a moment in time where the human soul releases itself from its interior "place" to create this physical "space" that binds human beings together into solidarity—like Hip-hop does.

In Chapter 3 of the book *Extraordinary Anthropology: Transformation in the Field,* Barbara Wilkens describes "space" and "time" in the following way:

> "Space refers to a specific physical location in an environmental context. Place denotes an inherently reciprocal position in the relational order of family, community, and the larger global village. When space, place and time come together, the value

of wholeness that ensures that if all do their part, social order, harmony and balance will be achieved."[91]

I believe that this approach was the original intention of Jesus' public ministry; a ministry that was constantly putting His life into jeopardy. Yet He remained resilient, and took chances, because He knew that that pain, emotion and violence would soon be accompanied by His passion for hope, justice and love. Hip-hop, like Jesus Christ, has faced scrutiny at many levels, particularly with the media, academia and the Church. However it too remains resilient, upholding its criticism of the injustices that are destroying our world.

This sort of "cosmic consciousness," or what I perceive to be the Spirit of God, is the reason that Hip-hop culture, from its outset, has embraced public ministry. Like Jesus, the Hip-hop culture has utilized public discourses as platforms for encouraging change in both the individual and society at large. Whether through protest, community forums, workshops, providing jobs and/or trainings for future community activists, etc., Hip-hop is *the* quintessential breeding ground for social grassroots movements of the twenty-first century, for both the church and socio-political arenas.

Professor Roger Haight and Shawn Madigan, whom I referred to earlier in this book, agree that the church (prayer, worship and liturgy) and its spirit do in fact encourage humans to take action in all aspects of politics, education, laws and the community. In the book, *Spirituality Rooted in Liturgy*, Shawn Madigan describes worship as being "a pattern of cultural and counter-cultural"[92] development. If this is the case, then worship—in part—has its relevance in social action in the same way that emotion "encourages us to *act* in conformity with it."[93]

One of the most frequently asked questions in my *Social Ethics as Social Criticism* class was: What do we do with this newfound knowledge? In other words, how do we go from public discourses to practicality? I would like to pose the same questions to Hip-hop culture because Hip-hop

---

[91] Jean-Guy Goulet and Bruce Miller, eds., *Extraordinary Anthropology: Transformation in the Field* (London: University of Nebraska Press, 2007), 77.

[92] Madigan, 92.

[93] Roberts, 22.

is more than just music videos, radio play, misogynistic overtones and glorifying material wealth—it is also about social change.

For example, MC and philosopher KRS-One, in collaboration with his Temple of Hip-hop, has been running a "Stop the Violence Movement"[94] campaign since 1989. This initiative, which consists of dialogue, conflict resolution and peace culture among youth, began with a song entitled *Self-Destruction*. Here is an excerpt from the song by Hip-hop legend, Doug E. Fresh:

> This is all about, no doubt, to stop violence/
> But first let's have a moment of silence/
> Things been stated re-educated, evaluated/
> Thoughts of the past have faded/
> The only thing left is the memories of our belated/ and I hate it/
> When someone dies and gets all hurt up/
> For a silly gold chain by a chump; word up!/
> It doesn't make you a big man/
> And to want to go out and diss your brother man/
> And you don't know that's part of the plan/
> Why? Cause rap music is in full demand/
> Understand!/[95]

Various other social change movements can be seen in the same place where Hip-hop started—in the South Bronx. One of those I have mentioned numerous times throughout this book is Youth Ministries for Peace and Justice (YMPJ). YMPJ has been at the forefront of various social change projects; some of which include the preservation of wildlife in the Bronx River, providing GED classes for youth, and planting trees to

---

94 The Stop the Violence Movement (STVM) is a non-profit organization deeply rooted in the Hip-Hop community with a mission to advance an ongoing series of movements to diminish global violence through education, critical dialogue, grassroots organizing and direct action. The STVM achieves its mission by providing organized programs, workshops, symposiums and media campaigns that heighten the awareness of the effects of violence, create multi-generational dialogue and supplies parent and youth oriented educational tools for conflict resolution.

95 KRS-One, *Self-Destruction,* Self-Destruction 12", Jive Records, 1989.

offset the excessive pollution that causes high rates of asthma in the South Bronx.[96]

We see the same social justice initiatives in other previously mentioned churches, such as Search and Rescue in Rhode Island, Catalyst Miami in Northwest Miami, Holy Hood in the South Bronx and Tha House in Chicago. All of these churches continue to be inspired to act by Jesus' "Word," spirituality, and emotion, because they are all working for a transformation of not just their own communities, but of the world.

The Praise Tabernacle Church bus, which picks homeless people off the streets of Downtown Providence to attend worship service.

The churches that first appeared in the Mediterranean in the first century soon spread into areas beyond its borders to the "Other" world. Similarly, Hip-hop's churches spread beyond the South Bronx and into other places and spaces around the world.

In the beginning of January of 2009, I traveled to Colombia in South America to study Peace Culture and Peace Movement with a group of my colleagues from Union Theological Seminary in New York City. This travel seminar was facilitated by Professor Chung Hyun Kyung, an Associate

---

[96] For further discussion on this topic, please see Chapter 1.

Professor of Ecumenical Studies, and Amada Benavides, Director of the School of Peace in Medellín and Bogotá, Colombia.

Me performing for a chapel service at Union Theological Seminary at Columbia University.

Throughout our two weeks spent there, we met with various individuals and organizations that are committed to the implementation and preservation of peace culture and peace education in Colombia. This immersion course exposed me (and my colleagues) to a beautiful country whose history not only consists of armed struggle, government corruption, racism, internal displacement (as a result of land disputes) and gangs, and a myriad of other social disorders, but also a country that has embraced a culture of peace, education, hope, community organizing, justice, faith, love and God.

One of the most powerful elements in this peace cultural movement has been the youth in Colombia. According to statistics from the School of Peace (our hosts in Colombia), almost half of the population of Colombia is between the ages of 10 and 20. Therefore, it is primarily the youth who are being impacted, directly and indirectly, by the armed struggle of this country.

Given this reality, it is no surprise to hear that countless youth—both men and women—throughout the barrios of Colombia have stories to share about a culture of drugs and violence that has killed family members or friends. Some of these stories speak about the paramilitaries kidnapping a neighbor or a cousin being displaced as a result of guerrilla pressure to either join up or be relocated, and countless other atrocities. When faced with this kind of violence and uncertainty, youth become more vulnerable, to the temptations of a life of fast money, cars and protection versus a life of poverty and fear.

Because so many youth are being affected by the realities of life in Colombia, a high level of resistance is underway in order to provide these youth an alternative to gang life and military violence. These alternative measures can be seen throughout the city on street corners, on the walls of not-for-profit organizations, and expressed in the public and private universities.

Youth B-boying in Medellin, Colombia in South America.

But where we see this resistance and cultural peace movement mostly happening is in the Hip-hop culture. For youth living in the Colombian context, Hip-hop culture is not just viewed as another form of entertainment and leisure, but also as a way of saving peoples' lives.

According to Alejandro, a.k.a. Alejo, "this music unites the different ethnic groups of Colombia (Black, White and Indigenous) while drawing the youth into an alternative lifestyle that is beyond what they see on a daily basis." In other words, the culture of Hip-hop becomes a bridge for the various potentials of youth, some of which include the following: artistry (by way of graffiti), public speaking (by way of rhyming or MC-ing in front of small or large crowds) and through choreography/body coordination techniques (or B-Boying and B-girling).

These liberal arts tools allow for a new and inspiring avenue of expression for the youth, but one of the most important things I see Hip-hop doing is binding ethnic groups together, as Alejandro mentioned. When you consider that Afro-Colombians make up 60% of the population in the city of Choco and that 23% of all Colombians are indigenous, race relations becomes a vital component of Colombian culture.[97]

However, the significance of these budding alliances appears at times to be more opportunistic, considering the distrust projected by the paramilitaries, guerillas, the government and the civil police toward the general public. Because racism is such a problem in Colombia, places like the Cultural House Organization in Medellin have become popular places of sanctuary for young mestizo men like Alejandro. The Cultural House in Medellin not only became a place where he could "spit those rhymes," but also a place where he felt called to a unified peaceful cause, as opposed to the division propagated between armed militia groups.

The words of protest and emotion that come from the mouths of these youth is more than enough to assemble a plethora of MC's who can relate to the reality of life in Colombia and have a similar goal—to change it. As stated by Colombian politician Piedad Esneda Córdoba Ruiz, "the youth are the key to the liberation of Colombia!"

And so, it is the experiences of these youth combined with their lyrical abilities, challenges and injustices that allow "the rubber to meet with the road." This vital blend provides a space (like the Cultural House

---

[97] For further discussion on this topics, please see Frank Palacios and Marco Palacios, *Colombia: Fragmented Land, Divide Society* (Oxford: Oxford University Press, 2002).

Organization in Medellin) for youth to have a voice, or a public testimony (discourse), regarding the affects of the armed conflict in their own respective neighborhoods.

Essentially, it is in this Colombian context that Hip-hop is being used by youth as a medium to convey words of pain, lucha (struggle), and hope. By recognizing their common struggle (e.g. armed conflict), race and socioeconomic status becomes no longer relevant. Instead, marginalized youth of Colombia are embracing Hip-hop as a way to change their social realities.

The impact that Hip-hop culture is having in Colombia can be seen in other parts of the world as well. For example, in France, Hip-hop music and culture has been appropriated by African and Arab teens to describe the political and economical disenfranchisement that they face on an almost daily basis, not to mention the ongoing racism they encounter in the various housing projects that exist in and around the city of Paris. Another example can be found in South Africa, where the most popular form of Hip-hop is called Kwaito,[98] Kwaito, which has seen growth similar to the Hip-hop movement in the United States, is a direct reflection of the post-apartheid environment in South Africa and is being used as a voice for the voiceless.

So, given this information, what can we say about the social and spiritual power of Hip-hop? It certainly creates a public discourse that resembles the churches of antiquity in the first century: community gathering, or "domestic houses," a meal, diversity, fellowship and a love for Jesus Christ. It also resembles many of today's churches, such as the Pentecostal church, because it celebrates spiritual gifts such as music, rhyming, free-styling (which resembles the gift of speaking in tongues), worship, liturgy, prayer and finally, a charismatic-like emotion that instigates a call for action.

---

[98] For further discussion on this topic, please see Dipannita Basu, Sidney Lemelle, Robin Kelley, *Vinyl Ain't Final*: Hip-hop and the Globalisation of Black Popular Culture (Ann Arbor, Michigan: Pluto Press, 2006).

From left to right: Rowland, Danny AKA Mystery, Me, and Majesty.

In reality, Hip-hop is a medium that can be used as an alternative to, not necessarily a replacement for, the institutional churches, because it does something that the church does not always do: it creates a space for public discourse regarding the injustices that are affecting that community. From this space we can see a spirituality from "below," that is, from society's vantage point, develop and inspire young men and women to change their own social realities.

Me presenting in front of the World Council of Churches as part of the Ecumenical Water Network initiative in Bossey, Switzerland.

Unfortunately many churches, clergy men and women, institutions of higher learning and youth ministry programs disapprove of Hip-hop's culture. The problem is that those individuals and institutions have never taken the time to actually *listen* to what some of our disenfranchised youth have to say. Unbeknownst to them, Hip-hop is in fact changing the lives of millions of youth all over the world—including myself.

Throughout my many years of listening, observing and participating in the Hip-hop culture, I can honestly say that *my* culture, Hip-hop, has a lot to say about, well, everything! But if I were to summarize everything that our youth *are* saying through the Hip-hop culture, both in and out of the church, I would say that youth are seeking the following:

1. Our leaders and mentors should not only punish us for wrongdoing, but encourage us when we are doing right.

2. We need to focus more on community building (churches) and community dialogue. This includes teaching young people to work together and support one another in social, political, economical and religious movements.

3. Young people need to be taught from a place that reflects our daily lives and struggles. This means teaching us the realities of history, not just the Eurocentric romanticism that our schools are currently feeding us.

4. We need to improve the quality of teachers in urban public schools. This implies developing a system where young minority students can receive the same quality of education as white students in well-funded suburban and urban schools.

5. We need to recognize the emotional needs of the youth.

6. It must be understood that we want a world where racism, sexism, classism, oppression, and social and environmental injustice no longer exists.

7. And finally, we want to participate *fully* in the glory of God's work. In other words, we want to be part of the church and help *you* (the

church) to bring God's message into those places where you are failing—the streets. This means allowing us to participate not only in worship, liturgy and ministry, but also in the decision-making policies of the church!

These are but a few of the many demands that our youth are expressing via the Hip-hop culture. Consequently, the decision makers of this world *must* consider utilizing Hip-hop as another way of extending God's message "even to the least of these." Because the reality is, as long as there is struggle, injustice and oppression, Hip-hop will live on to resist those inequalities by bringing God's hope into the mouths and hearts of these street disciples.

So the next time you see youth "spitting those rhymes" on your street corner, just remember that church is in session, and that God's spirit is working in these youth and inspiring them to change the world. And all God's people said, "Amen!"

EPILOGUE

There are rare moments in the life of a dying mainline Protestantism that give me hope. The consistent imperial considerations of religious leaders serve to only hinder the re-emergence of a prophetic church in late modernity. Moreover, the romantic predictions by several observers that Hip-hop is the alternative to, or progenitor of, moral malaise beset the urban condition has proven to be wrong on both accounts. The elegant treatment of Hip-hop as essentialist claims by Walter Hidalgo represents a fresh approach to the challenges faced not only by the church, but also of our beleaguered democracy. His text pushes us to consider the very nature of what it means to be church and who has the right to do theology.

In the best of the philosophical traditions of Paulo Freire, James Cone and his own beloved mother, Hidalgo situates "the least of these" at the center of our theological imagination and sources them as theological authorities. By highlighting the positive and consciousness raising lyricists, and the deep existential musings of the Hip-hop artist, we are taken on a tour de force of the eloquence that emerges from the ugliness so often hidden in our democratic dialogue. By pointing to the emerging trends and tracing the religious trajectory of Hip-hop, we encounter a generation wrestling with the most fundamental ideas about life and life chances. They are forming and shaping a theology of existence in the face of bleak prognoses. Hip-hop was born in the Bronx; on the tongues of globalized, transnational, urban poor bodies in de-industrialized and divested spaces. The shear devastation of the city became the place that the most innovative musical genre of the last generation would be conceived. At the least, Hip-hop pioneers embodied the hope and angst of the city; at their best, they were able to re-imagine the possibility of their humanity through lyrics.

Hidalgo constructs a project that hones the genius of Hip-hop in a way that pushes us to understand that Hip-hop does not *need* the salvation of the church; instead, Hip-hop just may be its greatest salvation.

Reverend Osagyefo Sekou
Author of "Gods, Gays, Guns: Religion and the Future of Democracy" and
Associate Fellow for Religion and Justice at the Institute for Policy Studies

BIBLIOGRAPHY

Adaso, Henry, ed., *A Brief History of Hip-Hop and Rap.* [database-on-line]. Available from http://www.about.com. Accessed 8 December 2008

Ahmed, Nora Sam and Sanchez, Jose, ed., *From Bronx High School Teachers.* [database-on-line]. Available from http://www.worldcantwait.net. Accessed 8 December 2008.

Basu, *Dipannita and Lemelle, Sidney and* Kelley, *Robin, Vinyl Ain't Final*: Hip-hop and the Globalisation of Black Popular Culture. Ann Arbor, Michigan: Pluto Press, 2006.

Berger, Teresa, *Dissident Daughters: Feminist Liturgies in Global Context.* Louisville, Kentucky: Westminster John Knox Press, 2001.

Brenner, Martha, *Emergency Asthma: Clinical Allergy and Immunology.* New York: *Marcel Dramatist Ltd*, 1999.

Brown, Robert McAfee, *Spirituality and Liberation: Overcoming the Great Fallacy.* Philadelphia: The Westminster Press, 1998.

Burgess, Stanley M. and Van Der Maas, Eduard M., eds., *The New International Dictionary of Pentecostal and Charismatic Movements.* Grand Rapids, Michigan: Strang Communications Company, 2002.

Campos, Leonaldo Silveria, ed., *In the Power of the Spirit: The Pentecostal Challenge to Historic Churches in Latin America.* Arkansas City: CELEP, Douglas Peterson, 1996.

Caro, Robert, *The Power Broker: Robert Moses and the Fall of New York.* New York: Vintage Books, 1974.

Chang, Jeff, *Can't Stop, Won't Stop: A History of the Hip-hop Generation.* New York: St. Martin's Press, 2005.

Common, *One Day It'll All Make Sense*, Relativity Records, 1997.

Cone, James, *The Spiritual and the Blues.* New York: Orbis Books, 1972.

DMX, *It's Dark and Hell is Hot*, Def Jam/Ruff Ryders Records, 1998.

Doogers, Andre. *More Than Opium: An Anthropological to Latin American and Caribbean Pentecostal Praxis.* Maryland: Scarecrow Press, Inc., 1998. Farrell, Amy and McDevitt, Jack "Rhode Island Traffic Stop Statistics Act Final Report," *Northeastern University Institute on Race and Justice,* 31 December 2002, *Data Collection Resource Center.* Database on-line; accessed on March 3, 2009.

Flanagan, Kieran, *Sociology in Theology: Reflexivity and Belief.* New York: Palgrave Macmillan, 2007.

Fraser, David A. and Campolo, Tony, *Sociology: Through the Eyes of Faith.* New York: HarperCollins Publishers, Ltd., 1992.

Fricke, Jim and Ahearn, Charlie, eds., *Yes Yes Y'all: The Experience Music Project Oral History of Hip-Hop's First Decade.* New York: Da Capo Press, 2002.

Gerberding, R. and Cruz, J. H. Moran, *Medieval Worlds.* New York: Houghton Mifflin Company, 2004.

Goulet, Jean-Guy and Miller, Bruce, eds., *Extraordinary Anthropology: Transformation in the Field.* London: University of Nebraska Press, 2007.

Gutiérrez, Gustavo, *A Theology of Liberation.* New York: Orbis Books, 1988. Grandmaster Flash and the Furious Five, *The Message,* Sugar Hill Records, 1982.

Haight, Roger, *Christian Community in History: Volume 1, Historical Ecclesiology.* New York: The Continuum International Publishing Group, Inc., 2004.

Hager, Steven. *Hip Hop: The Illustrated History of Break Dancing, Rap Music, and Graffiti.* New York: St. Martin's Press, 1984.

Harrington, Daniel J. and Keenan, James F., *Jesus and Virtue Ethics: Building Bridges between New Testament Studies and Moral Theology.* Maryland: Rowman and Littlefield Publishers, Inc., 2002.

Holness, Lyn and Wustenberg, Ralf and Grutchy, John, eds., *Theology in Dialogue: The Impact of the Arts, Humanities, and Science on Contemporary Religious Thought.* Grand Rapids, Michigan: William B. Eerdmans Publishing Company, 2002.

Howard-Brook, Wes, *The Church Before Christianity.* Maryknoll, New York: Orbis Books, 2001.

Joel Ortiz, *The Brick: Bodega Chronicles*, Koch Records, 2007.

Johnson, Marilynn S., *Justice: A History of Police Violence in New York City.* Boston: Beacon Press, 2004.

Kanye West, *The College Dropout*, Roc-A-Fella/Island Def Jam Records, 2004.

Keating, James, ed., *Spirituality and Moral Theology: Essays from a Pastoral Perspective.* New York: Paulist Press, 2000.

Kelling, George and Coles, Catherine, *Fixing Broken Windows: Restoring Order and Reducing Crime in Our Communities.* New York: Martin Kessler Books, The Free Press, 1996.

Kitwana, Bakari, *The Hip-hop Generation: Young Blacks and the Crisis in African-American Culture.* New York: The Perseus Books Group, 2002.

Knight, Michael Muhammad, *The Five Percenters: Islam, Hip-hop and the Gods of New York.* Oxford, England: Oneworld Publications, 2007.

KRS-One, *Self-Destruction 12"*, Jive Records, 1989.

Laurentin, René, *Catholic Pentecostalism.* New York: Doubleday & Company, Inc., 1977.

Light, Alan, ed., *The Vibe History of Hip-Hop.* New York: Three Rivers Press, 1999.

Lindberg, Carter, *The Reformation Theologians: Introduction to Theology in the Early Modern Period.* Oxford: Blackwell Publishers, Inc., 2002.

Macionis, John J., *Sociology,* 2nd ed. New Jersey: Prentice-Hall, Inc., 1989. Madigan, Shawn, *Spirituality Rooted in Liturgy.* Washington D.C: The Pastoral Press, 1988.

McQuillar, Tayannah Lee and Brother J, *When Rap Music Had a Conscience: The Artists, Organizations and Historic Events that Inspired and Influenced the Golden Age of Hip-Hop from 1987 to 1996.* New York: Thunder's Mouth Press, 2007.

Morse, Christopher, *Not Every Spirit: A Dogmatics of Christian Belief.* Valley Forge, Pennsylvania: Trinity Press International, 1994.

Muhammad, Ashahed M., ed., "Hip Hop: The Voice of Youth and Social Activism," *FinalCall.Com News,* 07 August 2008. [database-on-line]. http://www.finalcall.com/artman/publish/article_5078.shtml Accessed 27 March 2009.

Nas, *Untitled,* Def Jam and Columbia Records, 2008.

Orozco, Lucia, ed., "Hip-Hop, Urban Lifestyle Meets a Higher Power." *Miami Herald,* NorthWest Miami Edition, 09 January 2009. [database-on-line]. www.miamiherald.com/news/miami_dade/northwest/story/844464.html Accessed 2 February 2009.

Palacios, Frank and Palacios, Marco, *Colombia: Fragmented Land, Divide Society.* Oxford: Oxford University Press, 2002.

Perry, Imani, *Prophets of the Hood: Politics and Poetics in Hip-Hop.* London: Duke University Press, 2004.

Potter, Andrew and Heath, Joseph, *Nation of Rebels: Why Counterculture Became Consumer Culture.* New York: HarperCollins Publishers, Ltd., 2004.

Price, Emmett George, *Hip-Hop Culture.* Santa Barbara, California: ABC-CLIO Inc., 2006.

Provine, Doris, *Unequal Under Law: Race in the War on Drugs.* Chicago: University of Chicago Press, 2007.

Rivera, Raquel, *New York Ricans from the Hip-Hop Zone.* New York: Palgrave Macmillan, 2003.

Robert, Roberts C., *Spirituality and Human Emotion.* Grand Rapids, Michigan: William B. Eerdmans Publishing Company, 1982.

Spencer-Jones, H.D.M., *The Early Christians in Rome,* 2nd edition. London: Metheun, 1911.

Spohn, William, *Go and Do Likewise: Jesus and Ethics.* New York: Continuum International Publishing Group, 1999.

The New Oxford Annotated Bible, Revised Standard Version. New York: Oxford University Press, 1973.

Townes, Elmer, *Putting an End to Worship Wars.* Tennessee: Broadman & Holman, 1997.

Valentin, Benjamin, *Mapping a Public Theology: Beyond Culture, Identity and Difference.* New York: Trinity Press International, 2002.

Watkins, Craig, *Hip-Hop Matters: Politics, Pop Culture, and the Struggle for the Soul of a Movement.* Boston, Massachusetts: Beacon Press, 2005.

Wilson, James Grant, ed., *The Memorial History of the City of New York from Its First Settlement to the Year 1892.* New York: New York History Company, 1893.

Wilson, Ken, *Jesus Brand Spirituality: He Wants His Religion Back.* Nashville, Tennessee: Thomas Nelson, Inc., 2008.

Wink, Walter, *The Powers that Be.* New York: Augsburg Fortress, 1998.

Wu-Tang Clan, *Wu-Tang Forever*, Loud/RCA/BMG Records, 1997.

Zimring, Franklin E., The Great American Crime Decline: Studies in Crime and Public Policy. New York: Oxford University Press, 2007.